A TREASURY OF EARLY AMERICAN HOMES

A Treasury of
EARLY AMERICAN HOMES

by RICHARD PRATT

Whittlesey House

McGRAW-HILL BOOK COMPANY, INC. · NEW YORK · LONDON · TORONTO

A TREASURY OF EARLY AMERICAN HOMES

PUBLISHED BY WHITTLESEY HOUSE

A division of the McGraw-Hill Book Company, Inc.

PRINTED IN THE UNITED STATES OF AMERICA

FOREWORD

THIS book was made possible by the previous publication in the *Ladies' Home Journal* of the twenty-two color-illustrated articles now brought together here between covers. For it would appear that only a magazine with millions of readers is able to undertake a project whose preparation costs alone—of research, travel, photography, and color engravings —would make this kind of a book by itself prohibitive in price. . . . So thanks to the *Journal's* editors, Bruce and Beatrice Blackmar Gould, who first put forth the idea of the Regional Series and then gave the book idea their backing, and to The Curtis Publishing Company, which freely donated the indispensable printing plates, we have "A Treasury of Early American Homes."

As the Goulds have previously written, "Here in this country, instead of palaces, temples, tombs, or cathedrals, the real historical monuments are the fine old homes that tell the history of our American people. They keep a personal and appealing record of the way people lived when the nation was young.

"The fascination they still have for people today is clearly shown by the large and ever increasing number of yearly visitors to well-preserved places like Charleston and Natchez; to the almost untouched tidewater sections of Virginia and Maryland, where organized pilgrimages are made every spring; and to restorations like that most remarkable one at Williamsburg. Also, by the enthusiastic way the Regional Series, brought together in this book, has been received by readers of the *Ladies' Home Journal*.

"Perhaps a thousand exemplars of these fine old houses still survive, along with many minor examples, out of ten times as many in which people once lived and made our history. Fire, storm, and war have done much of the devastating. Periods of poverty and neglect have destroyed others. But the ones remaining indicate that the houses which have disappeared might still be standing if it were simply a question of their original strength and durability. They were built to last.

"This new interest in our heritage homes is a hopeful sign that the houses which are left will be encouraged to keep on living as beautifully as they appear in these pages."

An attempt has been made to place the houses here in historical sequence, separating them at the same time into three major sections like scenes in a play. All of which I hope will meet with the approval of any expert in the audience, who I am sure will be the first to see that the performance here has been planned not only for enlightenment but for entertainment in particular. And I think it is safe to say that as far as this visual pleasure is concerned, no book has ever before even begun to depict our country's early golden age of houses so effectively and faithfully in color. By that token, its intention, whatever it may teach, is clearly one of pure enjoyment.

I feel that I can speak this way because in a sense it was merely my good fortune to be on hand at the opportunity of a lifetime. It was like being let into a fabulous cavern of treasures from which I was enabled to emerge, month after month, with my arms as full as I could hold them. . . . What was it like? The question came up in various ways. How did we find all these houses in the first place? How did we get permission to use them after we had found them? And how did we go about photographing them?

Although I have spent most of my life scrutinizing houses, old and new, the search for and the selection of many houses here turned out to be more of a task than I'd expected. For the problem was not simply to get together the great houses and the good houses of the past, but to get them *looking* great and good. And sad to say, many remaining originals of once rare distinction are now ruins of neglect, disaster, and regrettable alterations. Time after time I have at last come face to face with a once beautiful old house only to find it either pitifully down-at-heels, wretchedly remodeled, or furnished completely out of character. Happily, however, the book bears witness to countless houses that have never looked better in their lives.

Quite a few of the houses were old acquaintances when the work began; others I already knew by reputation, and some turned up in searches among past periodicals, pictures, and books (see the Bibliography, page 134). Suggestions from friends and readers were frequently most fruitful; and the rest came to light in the course of looking over localities famous for their early architecture. You could never be altogether sure; but a clue was a clue, and you tracked it down, by plane, train, car, and occasionally on foot. And sometimes your breath, which you were holding, was taken away by what you saw.

Permission to photograph and publish had to be obtained rather delicately at times. For one thing, you could never be certain until you had looked a house over, inside and out, whether it was going to be suitable for pictures. It was only polite to let people know you were coming, and only fair to tell them that the first visit was frankly exploratory. A few owners were disinclined even to let me take a look, and while I could never quite see eye to eye with them on their reasons for this attitude, I could at least remind myself how I might feel if someone were to drive up to my door on a similar errand. In the case of a house I was eager to use, it was ordinarily enough, when faced with refusal, to point out the pleasure that millions of people all over the country would miss. As it turned out, I am glad to say that every house I tried to get is now safely in the book.

Reluctance lessened, of course, as the series progressed, and people became familiar with the kind of presentation we were making. But reluctance was never the rule; quite the opposite. In the case of houses now open to the public as living museums we were welcomed with open arms. At the Whipple house; the Wythe; the Hammond-Harwood and the mansions in Fairmount Park; the Tapping-Reeve; Monticello; the Peirce-Nichols and the Pingree, the people in charge couldn't have been more cordial: they put the keys in our hands, placed themselves at our disposal, and made the privilege in every way a pleasure.

When it came to the houses that were privately owned, the privilege was perhaps even greater for its being of a more personal nature. For photographing rooms in color can play hob with the habits of the household. But if I ever detected a sign of impatience on the part of an owner, even of one who was reluctant to start, it escapes me now.

In any event, after arrangements had been made, a station wagon would drive up, loaded to the roof, and a photographer and his assistant would begin discharging huge cases of equipment at the door. Another car or two would arrive containing sundry helpers, me, and boxes of flowers. And I hasten to insert that on many occasions especially valuable assistance contributing to the pictures' full effectiveness was furnished by my wife. Her advice was sound, her eye quick to catch the easily overlooked details, her feminine first aid invaluable in quite a few emergencies. When she was there, time counted for twice as much, in every way.

At any rate, here we were; and while cameras, floodlights, and cables were being unpacked and put together, while a technical assistant with a torch was locating electric connections in the cellar, and cartons of flowers were being uncovered, the camera angles were studied, room by room, and scheduled to catch the sunlight as it moved around from window to window. Then, with picture positions planned, floodlights were maneuvered into place and the first room would be readied for its most becoming pose.

Without going into more of these details than might add interest to the pictures that follow, it is enough to say that in rearranging any given area the purpose was always to bring out the flavor and personality of the room as faithfully as possible, giving to the fixed stare of the camera the final effect of a roving eye. In quite a few cases this meant moving furniture, rugs, pictures; taking some pieces out entirely, and now and then substituting articles from other parts of the house. Owners who allowed themselves to witness the operation often winced, but under the spell of the floodlights and in the general confusion of cables, cameras, and panting personnel, they assumed, outwardly at least, an attitude of calm toward what must have seemed to them at times rather ruthless activities on our part, falling in, almost always, with the spirit of the proceedings. In fact, there was more than one instance when, after the picture was taken, rather than let us return the room to its original state, they would ask us to leave everything as we'd fixed it for the photograph—liked it better that way.

During these goings on indoors, I would keep one eye on the sunlight outside, and when the light was right I would tear myself away and take up my own camera to get pictures of the house or the town. This was perhaps a selfish intrusion into the province of the professional cameraman; but it was a temptation I couldn't resist. Nor could anyone else, I am sure, have resisted it who ever had a chance to place his head under a focusing cloth and see the glowing images of these unforgettable houses and their glamorous settings on the ground glass of a big eight-by-ten.

Weather was our worst enemy, but most of the time we were extremely lucky. The essential thing was sunlight, and if it wasn't there, we simply had to wait for it—which, in a place like New Orleans, where it rained for days, was no particular hardship. Summertime, in general, had certain disadvantages. The heaviness of the foliage could not only obscure the house from without but rob us of the indoor sunlight that we counted on to give the rooms a lively sparkle. In winter owners were often away and the house was closed up; the scene outside was apt to be bleak; and while a setting in the snow was something we always hoped to get, we were never able to time it right, which is why this one picturesque aspect fails to appear.

With a few exceptions, all our pictures were therefore taken in the spring and fall. Then, either the early buds were breaking, or the foliage was thinning out and turning on its autumn tints; the grass was green, there were flowers in bloom, and the sunlight was soft and slanting. Though I wonder now why we were so concerned about surrounding effects—the houses were sufficiently wonderful by themselves, regardless.

RICHARD PRATT

CONTENTS

For Dorothy

INTRODUCTION

THE story of American houses must begin without a single house to illustrate the start. For not one dwelling survives today which we can be sure was built before 1650, leaving the years running back to the settlement days of Jamestown and Plymouth unaccounted for by any examples still standing. But while from that curtain-raiser period of the Colonial show no props remain, fragments of information we have. A few foundations have been uncovered, there are written records, and plenty of sound surmises of what went on in the way of building; so that altogether we can fill in a fairly accurate picture.

The picture is quite austere, to say the least. For during the first few years after 1607 in Virginia, and after 1620 in Massachusetts, our Cavaliers and Pilgrim Fathers kept house in the rudest kind of huts and caves. Architecture as such was simply not a thing to which they could turn their attention right then; emergency building was as much as they could manage. But you can be sure that the minute they could get around to it they began to build with a need for greater comfort and protection, and an understandable wish for more convenience. With one eye on the Indians and the other on the architecture of their native land, they began to build for beauty too. Once provided with the tools and the time to use them, and with essential furnishings and fittings from England, these pioneers were putting up houses that from all accounts would have made most effective pictures with which to open these pages. Lacking examples, it is at least safe to assume from all we can learn that any prior houses built for permanence were very much like the ones with whose pictures we do in fact begin. From this beginning we run into richer and richer profusion; and while innumerable houses that would have been wonderful to show exist no longer, there are plenty to illustrate the tale, with many splendid and important examples to spare. But the profusion of fine architecture begins to peter out this side of the nineteenth century's romantic middle. There this story ends and another begins.

The houses, then, that are covered by this book, were built within the two hundred years between 1650 and 1850. All of them, from Woodstock and Portsmouth south to Charleston (except of course the ones in Natchez, New Orleans, and Monterey), were erected within the region of the English-controlled Colonies along the Atlantic seaboard, though many went up, as the section on the Young Republic shows, after that control was lifted by the Revolution. Certain of these later houses indicate the effort that was made during the early days of our independence to shake off, architecturally at least, our cultural ties with England; and how successfully or unsuccessfully this was accomplished, we shall see. As far as American Provincial is concerned—meaning Louisiana, Mississippi, and California—it will be apparent that there were at work in these then remote places other architectural influences than those stemming directly from England—notably Spanish and French. Yet in all the houses covered by this book there are features, whether faint or strongly marked, which reveal a close connection to the English family tree of architecture.

To see behind the beauty of the houses that follow, let us first take a look at that most prolific tree which did so much to produce this beauty. For from it were brought the seeds out of which these new American houses sprang, to multiply and flourish in our fresh and fertile soil. . . . Planted deep and long ago in the architectural loam of England, the tree grew up from medieval roots. Onto this traditional tree the English from time to time would graft cuttings gathered abroad—from Italy, Greece, and across the Channel. This had a very happy and healthy effect on English houses and provided a variety of building manners—Gothic, Renaissance, Classical—all of them quickly acquiring an English accent. So it was only natural that English settlers coming to America should speak, as it were, their native architectural tongue. It was only natural, too, that descendants of the settlers, for generations after, should inherit a taste for English styles and be prepared to propagate here any that came into being back home.

Thus Early Colonial may now be looked upon in the light of

1

historical building methods and fashions funneled through what was then held by most Americans to be the Mother Country. And by glancing back at the panorama of our past, which these houses adorn so handsomely, we can see how in their new environment all these homes of English breeding took on in time a character that became as American as the people who put them up and occupied them. The New Englanders remembered the humble Elizabethan cottages of the southeastern counties they had left behind; the new Virginians the larger and lesser houses nearer London. And those were quite accountably the homes they chose to emulate here throughout the formative years of the Colonies. They built from memory, and their memory was good, as anyone will agree who compares the surviving seventeenth-century houses of New England with the village architecture of Essex and Cambridgeshire, Surrey and Kent. Witness the Whipple house in the Ipswich chapter, whose prototype, for all I know, may still be standing somewhere back in Middlesex. And the same, with variations, holds true of the much smaller handful of existing seventeenth-century houses from Philadelphia south.

In several ways, however, it was impossible for the early colonists to translate literally from the architecture of the homeland, especially in New England, where the climate required more protection against both cold and heat than was needed in the more moderate seasons of southeastern England. Besides, here there was lumber galore, with which to board the walls against the weather. For while weatherboarding was by no means unknown in England, it was customary there to leave the framing timbers of the house exposed, filled between with brick and plaster; a style of structure that was at first tried here—and found wanting. Much, much later,—after 1850 and therefore beyond the scope and purpose of this present book—a half-timber craze did hit us hard. But that was a skin-deep style; had nothing to do with structure; had to do only with the romantic era, as of this moment just coming to a timely close, as many moderns hope. This half-timber madness, like many romantic fashions from 1850 to now, was a false face on the framing of a house; whereas in the seventeenth-century Colonies structure was something too vital to toy with. There were reasons of life and death why it had to be honest and right.

So for altogether functional reasons the early New England Colonists covered their cottages with clapboard and built enormous chimneys out of all traditional proportion to the size of the house, just as their fellow Colonists were doing further south. They made their windows smaller; not merely to help keep out the northern cold, but partly for the same reason that they whittled their hardware out of hickory and used pegs instead of nails; which was because of a fantastic tax on window glass and metalware, imposed by the Crown, like the tax on tea. But it was less obnoxious in the end, for soon, under cover, the Colonists began to make nails and locks and glass for themselves. They couldn't grow their own tea, but they could build their own houses, and their houses grew more and more American as the seventeenth century came to an end.

Elizabethan English was the flavor still, but the form and feel, the texture, the whole new look, were creating an architecture that was getting ready to declare its independence. You can call it Early Colonial. As an American style, loosely entitled the Cape Cod Cottage, its popularity has persisted, with few interruptions, right through to the present; living now primarily on what is left of its style alone and on the sentiment, surrounding it, of home, sweet home.

In the meanwhile, a new style was gaining ground in England. And because of the Kings in whose reigns it developed, it was known as Georgian. It was introduced from Renaissance Italy by Inigo Jones, and this famous English exponent of academic formality in architecture caused a fashion for pure form to supersede the medieval manner of building—a manner which had found its way here, as we have seen, to give our early Colonial houses their truly functional quality. Whereas the Renaissance style inaugurated in London by the celebrated Jones was another dish, decidedly; and as the houses in the second part of this book disclose, it was soon to appear on the American table.

But first it was to be adapted over there to something less monumental than palaces, public buildings, and vast country places. And in England, in the hands of Sir Christopher Wren, it became in that process one of the most gracious and becoming fashions ever applied to building, from manor houses down to modest dwellings. Its burst into popularity came at a most propitious time, following the great Fire of London; for on the face of the phoenix that rose from London's ashes the features were definitely and handsomely Georgian. And it wasn't long before those features became familiar in American façades.

Georgian came ashore at Williamsburg and spread up the James, as you will see from the pictures of Westover, the Wythe House, Carter's Grove, and Berkeley. It laid its loveliness on Charleston, Alexandria, New Castle, Philadelphia. It covered the Colonies with glory, especially where wealth and culture could give it their blessing. But though the responsibility was Wren's in a way, that architect never came in person to this country as has been rumored, nor was he ever the architect, *in absentia*, of any houses here.

The architects of this new style came here in bundles. They were books from London, inspired by the riches of the English Renaissance and filled with details carefully drawn, which Colonial craftsmen were quick to master. Handbooks for builders, their authors were men to remember and admire—William Halfpenny, Batty Langley, Robert Morris, William Pain, Abraham Swan. Our Later Colonial owes them its deepest debt of gratitude. For more doorways than you can mention, more mantels, windows, cornices, pediments, and paneling came straight from their pages than from any other source.

Many actual English craftsmen came as well, like Richard Bayliss and David Minitree for Carter's Grove, and William Buckland for Gunston Hall on the Potomac, and the Hammond-Harwood House in Annapolis. And of course these men spread the good work while they were here, helping the hands of Colonial carpenters and adapting the new architecture to Colonial towns and countrysides, and to the requirements of

Colonial owners as well. To the point, that, with the handbooks for assistance, almost any able builder could draw up and erect a Georgian house. Men of means and taste became architectural amateurs, and gave their Georgian homes a real American personality, as many of the pictures that follow here make plain.

So that by the time of the Revolution, the country's manners were architecturally mature. For Americans who liked to live the forthright simplicity of Early Colonial, a style of this kind had already been established. For those who preferred formality of plan and appearance, the Georgian style had been developed into a Later Colonial whose roots had taken kindly to our cultural soil. You could take your choice. For every Sandwich there was an Alexandria; for every Whipple house, a Westover.

But just as there can be no accounting for taste, there was no accounting, at this point in history, for the temper of the times; and by the time the Declaration of Independence was signed, the Revolution won, and the nation on its own, a change in both temper and taste was taking place. And it wasn't long before it began to show in our houses, particularly and at first in the homes of intellectuals, and most of all, and soonest, in the home of Thomas Jefferson at Monticello.

Jefferson was the most architecturally conscious statesman in the country—skillful and scholarly, and sternly devoted to the Classical style. That academic devotion had not only an aesthetic basis, but an emotional one as well; and on both scores he was scathing in his denunciation of Georgian design. The architecture of Williamsburg filled him with scorn; its prettiness seemed to him a parody of the only architecture worth while: the noble monuments of Greece and Rome. Emotionally he felt that Greece and Rome, apart from the beauty of their buildings, had much in common with our new United States; for they too, in their prime, had been young republics. And as a leader of this young republic here, a man of extraordinary parts and power, he was able to influence taste with great dispatch and wide effect. His own architecture is among the finest in the American past; but even more than examples of his work, like Monticello and the University of Virginia, his compelling passion for the Classical mode was the force that helped to change the tide of American taste.

Other forces were moving concurrently. And perhaps the most important of these were of English origin—bringing us back to that family tree. There was Lord Byron, for one, who with a poet's pervasiveness was making the world aware of the plight of Greece, then under attack by the barbarous Turks. And for another, there were the measured drawings that James Stuart and Nicholas Revett had made of Classical remains in Greece and Italy. These drawings appeared in London—great folios of engravings—adding fuel, as it were, to Byron's flames. That was all that was needed, not only to complete our identification here with those ancient other young republics, but to provide us with the means of reproducing here what seemed in the circumstances a most appropriate style of architecture. And the means of reproducing that architecture were facilitated by the appearance in London, and soon thereafter here, of builders' handbooks once again; but this time putting pure Classicism to work—at least as pure as possible, considering the transition that had to be made from ancient temples to contemporary houses, and from monumental masonry to domestic wood and plaster.

In the hands of Jefferson and a gathering group of able architects, this Classic urge produced a style of undeniable dignity, and in the later work of McIntire in Salem, and other architect-craftsmen elsewhere, it achieved a lush and eloquent beauty. It became for a while, in fact, what many consider the most authentically American manner of building, from mansions like Andalusia to templelike cottages. But as its popularity spread and the manner began to lose whatever meaning it had, the Greek Revival grew quainter and quainter, weaker and weaker. A Gothic revival, to become equally quaint, was coming to life in England; Ruskin was writing, and disciples here were stirring with new ideas. It was nearing 1850, and the Romantic Era was arriving, with an assortment of theatrical styles in which to disguise the Industrial Age. Early Colonial was having a relapse; Georgian was no longer liked; and the Classical Revival was subsiding. For fifty years or more to come, the houses collected here in this book were to be out of fashion, out of favor.

But before it was too late the twentieth century came to the rescue. Memories of our native architecture returned from distant periods of the past to please us once again. We began looking up the old houses, and in turn the old houses themselves began looking up; and as might have been expected, our new houses began looking more or less the way the old ones did in the early days. And while many have been undeniably handsome, nostalgia was not enough; the impulse of the real originals was missing, along with yesterday's necessities.

We have been building on borrowed architecture. Today's necessities, no longer new, are asking with greater and greater urgency for methods, materials, and means of production which rightly belong to the age in which we live today. And a new era in architecture is at last arriving.

Among the things to keep in mind while planning for the future are these houses of our inheritance. Perhaps in part they belong to the past, but in part perhaps to the present, too. At least let us hope that they will always haunt us with their beauty.

Queen Elizabeth (1533–1603)

The Medieval Look

in America

EARLY COLONIAL

Elizabethan Cottage

WHILE the first arrivals here to stay were tacking into coves and inlets up and down the coast, sailing up rivers and bays, with wonder in their eyes, Shakespeare was finishing "The Tempest," St. Peter's was being completed, Milton and Rembrandt were born, and Richelieu was the power behind the throne of France. On the map of America, place names were beginning to appear. Jamestown, Plymouth, Portsmouth, New Amsterdam, Salem, Marblehead, Boston; Dutch names up the Hudson, Scandinavian up the Delaware, and Indian names dotted all directions. Names of people, too, began coming into Colonial prominence: John Smith, Powhatan, and John Rolfe's celebrated bride, the legendary Pocahontas; Governor William Berkeley of Virginia; William Bradford, Myles Standish and William Brewster, of Mayflower fame, along with Endecotts, Carters, Winthrops and Mathers, Stuyvesants and Rensselaers, from Long Island to Albany, Johan Printz and Chief Tishcohan, where Delaware is now; Calverts and Claibornes, in Maryland; Lords Ashley, Berkeley and Craven in Carolina. And most of the names of places and people were English. . . . Things began to appear. By 1633 the first power sawmill was ripping logs into lumber on the Piscataqua. Settlers in 1611 at Jamestown were beginning to make brick, and shortly after, so were the Dutch at Albany and the Pilgrims in Massachusetts. Colonial glass began to take the place of oil paper for window panes; and tinsmiths and cabinetmakers were making household implements and furniture. The methods were medieval and went with the houses' medieval look.

The first English settlement in America was made at Jamestown four years after the death of England's spinster Queen. But already, to a New World region that was vast and vague, Elizabeth had given the name Virginia, thus commemorating the peculiar nature of her Royal person. To the period of her lengthy reign her name at home had been attached by bonds that never can be broken as long as language lives. And in the Elizabethan tradition lie not only the finest of poetry, but a method and manner of homebuilding whose effects will be felt as long as people live in houses. Very clearly, this effect can be felt in the houses that follow immediately in this first section of the book. These take in parts of three separate centuries: late seventeenth and eighteenth in New England; early nineteenth in Pennsylvania. All derive their functional form from a medieval manner and method of building which can today be found in the best of our contemporary domestic modern—a far cry now from those wilderness days and wilderness conditions that witnessed our earliest attempts at architecture.

North Church, an early example of wooden Gothic.

IPSWICH, MASS.

FOR seventeenth-century houses you can hardly do better than Ipswich—it being the claim of this charming old Massachusetts place that within the town itself, and along its outlying lanes, there are more of our earliest homes than anywhere else in the land. Not only do the houses send you back three hundred years to the time of the town's original settlers, but the Ipswich telephone book today gives you the names of those earliest families—descendants of a long line of local citizens whose enduring devotion to the place is of course the secret of the well-preserved appearance that Ipswich now presents. There may be slightly older houses elsewhere, but nowhere, to my knowledge, a more complete assembly of this pioneer period.

Every summer, in July, they celebrate a Seventeenth Century Day, and open all the historical homes to the public. But next to being there on that occasion, these six pages of pictures will give you the best idea it is possible to get of the beauty that was built into these first American houses. Their roots of style and structure stem from Elizabethan cottages of Southeastern England, from where the Pilgrims came; but here, in Massachusetts, because of a more rigorous climate and unlimited lumber, they took on at once a new American look. In them was born, thereby, a method and manner of building which is still going strong three centuries later, from here to every corner of the country coast to coast.

Ipswich River (facing page) rises and falls with the tide, through the town, bordered by ancient dwellings like the 1648 Emerson House that faces the old stone bridge.

Under the elms of High Street are the 1680 "House with the Orange Shutters," the Kimball House, built in 1715, and the gambrel-roofed Fowler House, 1720.

"Overhang" construction of east side of Whipple House and diamond-paned windows show colonists' liking for Elizabethan traditions.

This room was added as a kitchen in 1670. Early American ladder-back chairs face the widespread fireplace with its customary accouterments.

WHIPPLE HOUSE

THIS is without any question one of the very first houses to have been built in the English-speaking colonies of America, still standing to-day; the Ipswich chronicles setting forth that as early as 1638, a century and a half before the Revolution was won, John Fawn, a Pilgrim settler, began construction on this site. It might even now be known as the Fawn house, had Fawn unfortunately not sold his property within a couple of years. But it was bought and brought to completion by John Whipple, whose name it bears, and whose family and descendants occupied it for the next two centuries; at that, not a record for Ipswich, where another family, the Goodales, still live in the house their forebears built *three* centuries ago. At any rate, for reasons of age and quality, the Whipple House must be reckoned one of the most important in the country; being now preserved as a museum by the Ipswich Historical Society, which has furnished it with many fascinating pieces of the early period, and maintains it with meticulous care. Under those circumstances it should be standing for centuries to come; for after one look inside you can see that it was built to last. Its post-and-beam construction has grown even more solid and secure than it was when first put together; while this hardwood framing, dominated by the tremendous "summer" that supports the ceiling joists, gives the rooms an air of medieval strength and permanence. The roof and weatherboarding may have to undergo minor repairs every half century or so, but the essential body of the house is good enough to last forever.

From its position on the northeast corner of the Village Green where the local militia trained for King Philip's War one hundred years before the American Revolution, this old house has seen the march of many men playing their parts in succeeding chapters of American history. Few houses have witnessed so much, and fewer still look so well today anywhere.

The woodwork of the bedroom is the earliest in the house. Eighteenth-century field bed, with fish-net canopy, has a cross-and-crown coverlet woven in 1750.

LANGDON WARNER

Exterior is distinguished by a salt-box profile, with a hewn overhang on three sides.

CURIOUSLY enough, this house on the outskirts of town, overlooking the meadows that run down to the dunes and the ocean, is not a native of Ipswich, but was brought here about thirty years ago from Newburyport, ten miles away. In its present foster location, where the passage of time seems almost imperceptible, it has found a home where its future is assured; partly because of its present owner, Dr. Langdon Warner, Professor of Oriental Art at Harvard, whose occasional Korean pieces blend beautifully into the early American setting.

The stairway in the entrance hall is one of the most outstanding features of this house, illustrating the transition between the completely enclosed early types and the open, more decorative examples that followed later on.

The original stairway is one of the finest and best-preserved late Seventeenth-century types. English, Oriental and Early American furniture blend harmoniously in the large, heavily beamed living room.

Originally, this long room at the rear of the house was divided into three rooms, with the kitchen occupying the middle section—bedroom and storeroom at either end.

DODGE HOUSE

ACCORDING to Ipswich history, this house was built as a wedding present for the Robert Paine, Jr., who was later to become an important figure in the witchcraft trials at Salem, thirty miles toward Boston from here. The young man had been graduated from Harvard just four years before—in the class of 1656!—and the house into which he moved at his marriage must have been one of the best in the neighborhood, now a few minutes' drive from the center of town. The excellent restoration was accomplished by the late Mrs. Robert Dodge, whose son is now the owner.

A welcome wedding present three centuries ago, or today, you will agree.

The bedroom contains a Sheraton four-poster and Early American hooked rugs.

PHOTOGRAPHS BY EZRA STOLLER

CONNECTICUT SALT BOX

Nestling back in from the coast line of Connecticut, and on all the way to Cape Cod, you will find the remnants and relics of these wonderful old houses from the 1600's; and occasionally, like this one here, an example so well preserved that it brings that far-off past right up to the present. You can be sure it is not the fault of the house when you find one in ruins, for only neglect and disaster have ever been able to damage or destroy them. The heavy oak with which they were framed has taken on the enduring strength of steel, and the massive single chimneys which furnish great open fireplaces for every room, upstairs and down, are built like the pyramids. Simple to the point of severity, these houses come by their beauty through honest construction.

The typical rear roof line of the 1690 Ogden house at Fairfield, like an old-fashioned salt container, gives these houses their name. The present living room was once the lean-to kitchen, its huge fireplace—center of domestic life—filled with cooking implements. Note the hand-hewn beams after 2½ centuries.

The bed in the principal bedroom is covered with a spread of linsey-woolsey—a homespun, colored with butternut dye. Early primitives decorate the walls, and a Chippendale child's chair stands by the fire.

During the Revolution, when the British landed at Fairfield and burned most of the town, the Ogden house escaped destruction probably because it was off the line of march to Danbury—the invaders' next objective.

The smaller bedroom, with its little canopy and bed chest, is also completely decorated with homespun fabrics. . . . The Ogden house is now in the fortunate possession of Miss Mary Allis.

The dining room contains many splendid examples of early American furniture, including the gate-leg table and the 1690 banister chairs against the wall. The principal items of furniture in this house date prior to 1750, and all retain their original finish.

Sandwich, Mass.

PICTURESQUE PREFACE TO OLD CAPE COD

THIS village, which lies half hidden off the main highway that hurries along past the elbow of the Cape, and on to Provincetown at the finger tip, is like a page torn out of the past—still clear, clean, fresh and beautiful. The native architecture that it shares with the rest of the Cape, but for which it provides a setting especially choice, is of course the most widely copied in the country. For every town in every state is familiar with various versions of the Cape Cod cottages that were built beside the curving lanes of Sandwich more than two hundred years ago—the imitations never quite matching the fine originals with which this town is filled. The sincerest form of flattery has likewise been heaped upon a special handiwork of this unassuming village— a handiwork as fragile as the houses were strong; for the glassware which originated here in the last century is now imitated far and wide, in vaster quantities than any other

glassware in the world. Elsewhere you can see Sandwich glass and houses of the Sandwich type, but here where they belong you can see them at their best.

The town clusters around the old mill pond in the picture below, then thins out through surrounding cranberry bogs and meadows over to the dunes that guard the Bay. The first permanent settlement on Cape Cod, its boundaries were established three hundred years ago by two no less legendary figures than Capt. Myles Standish and his assistant, John Alden. Daniel Webster was an habitué of the inn up the street which bears his name; and one of the first glass blowers brought from Europe to Sandwich was suspected of being the lost Dauphin of France. And on a quiet solitary morning there, it is easy to imagine that any one of those old characters might still be around, peering out of a window from behind a fabulous piece of Opalescent, Jade Green or Golden Ruby glass.

14

EXTERIOR PHOTOGRAPHS BY RICHARD PRATT. INTERIOR PHOTOGRAPHS BY HAROLD FOWLER.

The rare bowed roofs are framed like the ribs of ships.

One of the very earliest, this house has never been restored.

An original of familiar design, just over in Barnstable.

An unusual example of the two-story "three quarter" type.

This "Captain's house" is now owned by Mrs. Charles D. Cook.

The paneled living room was originally the kitchen.

MORE THAN TWO CENTURIES OLD, THIS HOUSE STILL KEEPS ITS STRENGTH AND BEAUTY

SANDWICH houses range in size from the tiny "one-quarter Capes" to what might be called the "full-Capes" or "Captain's houses"—like this one that stands on one of the highest knolls of the town. "Half-a-Capes" were houses two windows wide, with a chimney at the end; the owner always hoping the day would come when he could add the other half and convert his cottage into a proper house with a central chimney, such as this, which was built in 1730 as it stands today, commanding a view of the town—a monument to the skill of those early carpenters who framed their wooden houses, regardless of size, for the centuries.

16

Sparkling with priceless Sandwich lamps and vases, Mrs. Cook's sitting room has a remarkable Goddard chest of 1770, and early paper in reproduction.

The dining-room chairs are eighteenth-century Hepplewhite by Goddard of Newport. The glass, quite naturally, is Sandwich.

The guest bedroom, with its inside shutters, has early maple four-posters, hooked rugs, Windsor chairs and more Sandwich glass.

Unlike it at first glance, the house of Peter Place Cook is almost identical with that of his mother across the street.

The paneled bedroom meets up with modern paper.

Pointing up the purity of the fireplace wall.

QUAIL HOLLOW, BUILT BY THOMAS TOBEY IN 1724, IS STILL ONE OF THE MOST COLORFUL OF SANDWICH HOUSES.

ONE of the things you notice about the Cape Cod houses of Sandwich is the variety of colors they can wear. Even when paint has never been present on the shingled sides, years of weathering have placed most becoming natural pigments on the cedar, which paint manufacturers have now been able to simulate. And while the walls of most of the painted ones are white, with trim of green, steel blue or gray, others are painted red, pale green, gray, or yellow—like Quail Hollow here.

Nor is severity the rule inside. Many of the floors are gaily spattered with paint drops of green, red, yellow, blue. The walls are often brightly papered, as you can see, and even the unpainted paneling has a special brilliance of its own. And for all their purity and primness within—or perhaps because of it—the Sandwich houses accept gracefully the wisely chosen furnishing and decoration of almost any modest manner from contemporary back to the simple and forthright things which first occupied them when they were new.

The living-room paneling was discovered under old handmade laths, plaster and wallpaper; needing only cleaning and rubbing.

An unusually handsome heirloom piano fits nicely into this parlor, with its Terry clock and Staffordshire hunting figures.

BUCKS COUNTY
Pennsylvania

A land of rich farms and sturdy houses.

COUNTY LINE · *An unusually fine example of the white-plastered Pennsylvania stone house, this one has four distinct roof levels in line, in all likelihood denoting different stages of construction. Note fine rooster weathervane.*

PLEASANT VALLEY · *Buildings like this old farmhouse in the upper part of the county, recently restored, and like its magnificent masonry barn beyond, were all constructed of the stone from their immediate vicinity.*

UHLERSTOWN · *Up until twenty years ago, hundreds of barges a month, pulled by mules, passed under this bridge and through the lock beyond, and hamlets like Uhlerstown were leisurely ports of call, with inn and piers.*

UPPER TINICUM · *Now showing signs of occupation by settlers from the city, this plain white farmhouse, like many in its neighborhood, was plastered so as to keep the rain from seeping through its porous stone walls.*

BUCKINGHAM · *Only a Bucks County stone house could take the Victorian period in its stride, and wear so well an 1860 cornice above its 1790 walls, keeping its essential character intact. This one was restored recently.*

SPRINGFIELD · *The farther up the county you go, the more red barns you meet (and green and yellow too); the witch signs decorating their sides to ward off lightning, fire and other ill fortune, increase their picturesqueness.*

This mellow old manor house is Bucks County at its best. Built of what the county people call "tailored" stone, carefully cut and laid, its flat-arched windows and doorway, and its flanking wings at lower level, are signs of its pre-Revolutionary period, when stone houses began to replace the log cabins of the locality's earliest settlers. It is about a mile from New Hope and the Delaware, on the road to Doylestown, and in the section now most heavily resettled by many well-known newcomers from Broadway, Park Avenue and Wall Street, northeast some sixty miles—a geographical fact made hard to believe by such houses, so faraway-looking in time and place.

The great feature of the dining room at Ingham Manor, and a characteristic feature of most Bucks County houses built between 1750 and 1850 (which might be called Bucks County's period), is what they call the "walk-in" fireplace; the wide opening supported by a massive lintel log of oak which is faced by a simply molded mantel. A room such as this would originally have been the kitchen, too, of course, and the winter living room as well; the cooking done above and beside a wood fire on the hearth and in a cavelike oven in the chimney's back wall. The floor of Pennsylvania tiles is typical, and the homespun Swedish table cover is set with country ironstone.

AQUETONG . The walls and woodwork of Ingham Manor reflect the finest features of Bucks County architecture

It is altogether possible that the extraordinary pine paneling of the living room at Ingham Manor is the work of the shipwrights who settled along the Delaware in the early days, and who turned their hands to house carpentry when boatbuilding was slow, for it has many of the earmarks of their craftsmanship: its simplicity and robust scale, which match so well the sturdy cabinetwork of the big Pennsylvania Dutch wardrobe. Very appropriate in this somewhat primitive room are the two "country Chippendale" chairs, so called because they follow the famous style in almost rustic fashion. The figures are Pennsylvania "chalk"; the plates, Bucks County slip ware.

PHOTOS BY FOWLER

Papered, paneled and painted, the walls of the dining room give background variety to the Empire table, chairs and sideboard, together with an effect of greater size in which the large square sheet of mirror plays its part. While outside, from across the lane, as you can see below, size requires no assistance. The barn has typical Bucks County bigness and beauty, the house it belongs to, a very special stateliness along with its distinguished stonework.

MECHANICSVILLE

· The forthright simplicity of Bucks County interiors provides an ideal background for contemporary color schemes like those shown and for furniture that ranges from Early American to modern.

Here in the high-ceilinged hallway of the Mechanicsville house it takes strap hinges of really prodigious size and strength to carry the weight of the heavy full-height doors, whose whiteness is a wonderful foil to the olive-colored walls.

As you can see by the mantel of the Mechanicsville living room, early Bucks County carpenters had access to handbooks of Georgian details, which, as here, they often simplified. Note how well the room takes to gilt valances and lace.

The guest bedroom is furnished with effective simplicity: Sleigh bed and cloth-draped bedside table, plus two unseen chairs, and chest of drawers. The portrait is a primitive, and by the window are two Pennsylvania Dutch "Fracturs."

SOLEBURY · *Nobody built better in Bucks County than the Quakers, and the meetinghouses of the Friends are models of beautiful masonry and simple, generous proportions, as you can see.*

NEW HOPE · *One of the oldest and most colorful Bucks County towns along the Delaware, long famous for its painters, New Hope's color now is even heightened by its summer-theater atmosphere.*

Sir Christopher Wren (1632–1723)

LATER

COLONIAL

The Georgian Look in America

By 1700 the map of the Colonies was becoming quite noticeably spotted; a few Colonial-size cities, many towns, and hundreds of hamlets; but highways between them were hardly worth marking on the map. And some of the prominent early places had already begun to relinquish their first importance to newer communities nearby—Plymouth to Boston, St. Mary's City to Baltimore, Jamestown to Williamsburg. It was most of all at Williamsburg, Virginia's new Colonial capital, that the new look in architecture which was to give the eighteenth century its predominating flavor here, made its most auspicious bow. And the one big name behind the new style's Colonial debut was that of the architect most responsible for the style's development in England—Sir Christopher Wren. It has been said that certain Williamsburg designs may have come from the drawing board of the master himself, and there are certain buildings in the present Restoration, both reconstructed and original examples, whose appearance would lend weight to this conjecture. In any event, Wren's English work in the Georgian manner was the main aesthetic force behind the best American houses of the time. He had his hands full rebuilding London after the Fire, and his celebrated couplet, "If anyone calls, I'm designing St. Paul's,"

further indicates how much too occupied he must have been at home to take on any Colonial commissions. Fortunately for the quality of our Colonial architecture, however, there were many able artisans who could come over to interpret the style for which he was famous, and a host of builders' handbooks to guide the workmen here, as mentioned in the Introduction to this volume.

It was a century of elegance in Colonial architecture, and a century that saw the ascendancy of figures forever famous in American history—Franklin, Washington, Jefferson. Midway through it, Bach and Handel died, and Voltaire; Mozart and Rousseau lived their lives; Beethoven was born. Colonial culture on the loftier levels reflected the drawing rooms of London and the Continental salons. Colleges were springing up throughout the Colonies. Colonial craftsmen, in metal, glass, and wood, were producing objects, from tableware to furniture, as fine as any from abroad; creating collector's pieces for us to prize in present times. And in the minds of Americans the thought of political independence was taking hold. When it came, the effects were of course profound—on people's lives, our national career, and incidentally on our houses, as the final section will depict.

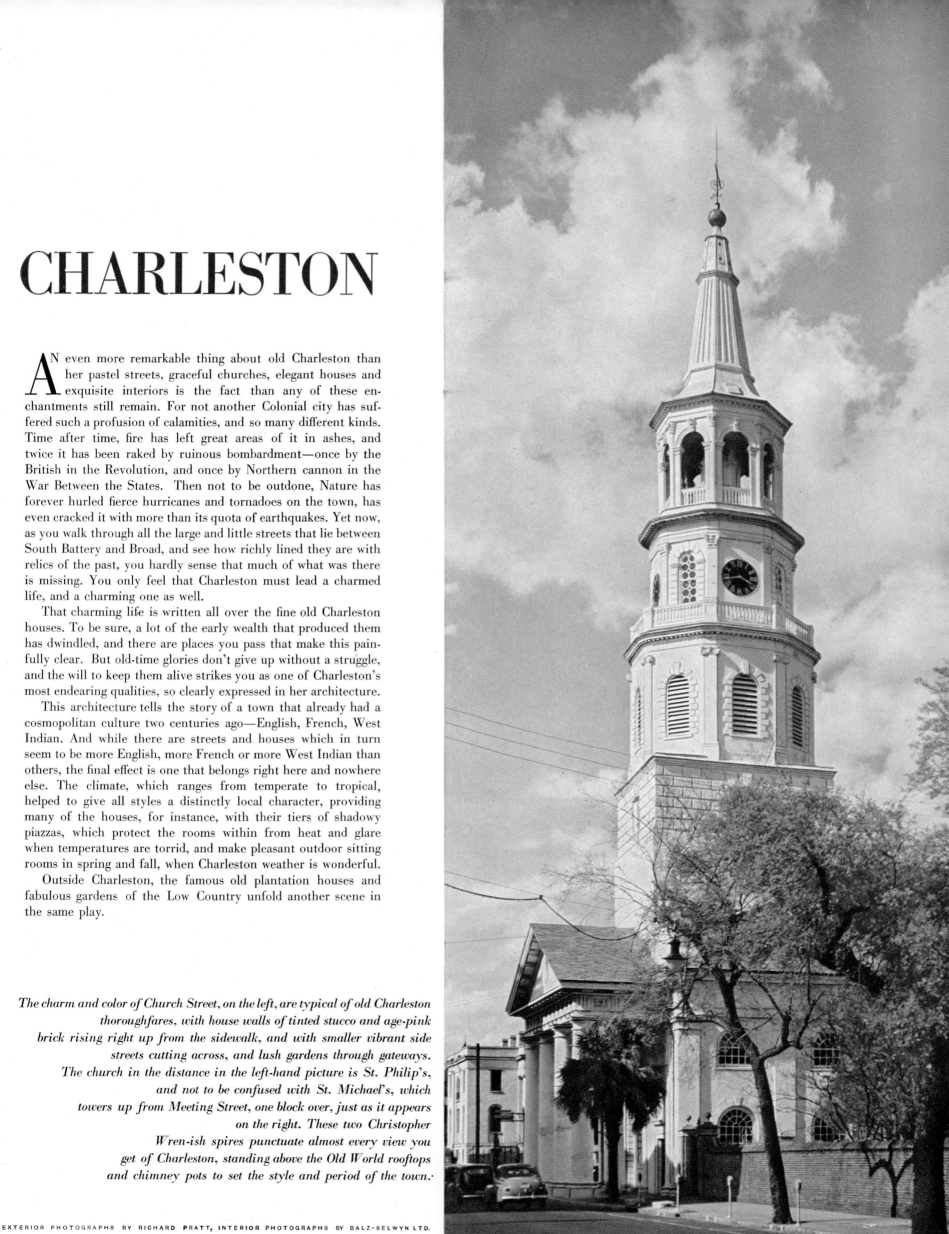

CHARLESTON

AN even more remarkable thing about old Charleston than her pastel streets, graceful churches, elegant houses and exquisite interiors is the fact than any of these enchantments still remain. For not another Colonial city has suffered such a profusion of calamities, and so many different kinds. Time after time, fire has left great areas of it in ashes, and twice it has been raked by ruinous bombardment—once by the British in the Revolution, and once by Northern cannon in the War Between the States. Then not to be outdone, Nature has forever hurled fierce hurricanes and tornadoes on the town, has even cracked it with more than its quota of earthquakes. Yet now, as you walk through all the large and little streets that lie between South Battery and Broad, and see how richly lined they are with relics of the past, you hardly sense that much of what was there is missing. You only feel that Charleston must lead a charmed life, and a charming one as well.

That charming life is written all over the fine old Charleston houses. To be sure, a lot of the early wealth that produced them has dwindled, and there are places you pass that make this painfully clear. But old-time glories don't give up without a struggle, and the will to keep them alive strikes you as one of Charleston's most endearing qualities, so clearly expressed in her architecture.

This architecture tells the story of a town that already had a cosmopolitan culture two centuries ago—English, French, West Indian. And while there are streets and houses which in turn seem to be more English, more French or more West Indian than others, the final effect is one that belongs right here and nowhere else. The climate, which ranges from temperate to tropical, helped to give all styles a distinctly local character, providing many of the houses, for instance, with their tiers of shadowy piazzas, which protect the rooms within from heat and glare when temperatures are torrid, and make pleasant outdoor sitting rooms in spring and fall, when Charleston weather is wonderful.

Outside Charleston, the famous old plantation houses and fabulous gardens of the Low Country unfold another scene in the same play.

The charm and color of Church Street, on the left, are typical of old Charleston thoroughfares, with house walls of tinted stucco and age-pink brick rising right up from the sidewalk, and with smaller vibrant side streets cutting across, and lush gardens through gateways. The church in the distance in the left-hand picture is St. Philip's, and not to be confused with St. Michael's, which towers up from Meeting Street, one block over, just as it appears on the right. These two Christopher Wren-ish spires punctuate almost every view you get of Charleston, standing above the Old World rooftops and chimney pots to set the style and period of the town.

The Staats House

This is one of the houses which survived the devastating fire of 1740, and stands on one of the very rare grants of land made by the Lords Proprietors to a woman, an Elizabeth Willis. Noteworthy, otherwise, for its most evident beauty, inside and out, it is fortunately built to last, with brick walls 29 inches thick, covered with oyster-shell stucco, and is paneled throughout with its original heart cypress. It also has a ghost, of a young poet who in 1786, outside the doorway, fought a duel over the famous actress, Perdita, and was brought inside the house to die. All very typically Charleston.

Within the white-paneled drawing room are rare pieces of Hepplewhite, Chippendale, Sheraton, an Adam mantel, an extraordinary old Tabriz animal carpet.

The color scheme for the dining room was taken from the Benjamin West portrait over the mantel; the chairs are Early American Regency made of mountain ash; the rug is an old floral needle point; and the camellias are from the garden.

Standing next to the old First Baptist Church, by Robert Mills, the house, now the residence of Mr. and Mrs. Henry Philip Staats, shows typical Charleston piazzas, the doorway leading into the lower piazza.

The Gibbes House

The face of the house is ornamented like an Adam mantel.

In the hallway, with its scenic paper, is a red Empire sofa.

. . . Facing out across the water from South Battery, it is amazing that this superb old mansion escaped injury from the bombardments of 1776 and 1861. It is one of Charleston's great residential monuments, the main floor standing a full story above the street, as though creating an excuse for the magnificent double staircase that decorates its Adamesque Georgian façade. Behind the house is a garden that glistens with white azaleas in the sunlight sprinkling down through the glossy leaves of great live oaks, and there are long, low servants' quarters and stables with shiny old tile roofs, so typical of Charleston.

The ballroom, which looks out across the Battery from the four right-hand windows of the top floor, is of course the showpiece of the house, but how to designate the showpiece of the ballroom is another matter: the spidery crystal chandelier? the immense Aubusson carpet? the plaster carving of the ceiling and cornice? . . . At any rate, other choice objects in the room are the early spinet and harp, rich brocades at the windows and on the furniture, and a gaming table said to have been used by Napoleon.

Wallpaper, decorations and even the English-detailed woodwork give the green drawing room (one of a pair on the main floor) a Chinese flavor.

Mulberry Plantation

Mulberry looks out over the Low Country from one of the locality's few hills.

THIS fascinating old house, of a most remarkable design, with four low corner towers, called flankers, of Jacobean baroque, and a generally sumptuous air, owes its opulence to the richness of the ancient rice fields down along the river. Its style and elegance can be credited to an early planter-politician, Thomas Broughton, who built it in 1714—some years before he really took title to the site; a lapse which causes local antiquarians still to raise their eyebrows.

But regardless of the manner in which Broughton acquired the property, the same authorities contend that as far as the house itself is concerned, the owner modeled it after the Broughton family seat in England. The old homestead must have been a house quite out of the ordinary, for Mulberry, as you can see, is not by any means the customary Colonial; in fact, it could be called unique. Principally, of course, because of the four little corner wings with their playful hoods above the lower hips, all topped with ornamental weather vanes. These wings, or flankers, have long been the cause of considerable controversy, one school of experts believing them to have some military significance, for the house did serve as a sort of fortress during various early wars with the Indians, and ancient cannon have been uncovered from what is now the lawn.

But other specialists point out that if these wings had been designed for defense, their large windows would have made them extremely vulnerable, even against arrows, and that slender slits in the brick would have offered more practical means of protection. At any rate, the flankers, for whatever they were meant, give the house great architectural charm, and provide breakfast room, study, office and pantry. The interior woodwork of the living and dining rooms is delicately Adam, and was probably installed by an owner in the early 1800's. The present owners have put the whole place in splendid condition—the lawns, walks, woods and waterside, as well as the house itself—and make Mulberry accessible in spring to the public as one of the loveliest relics of Low Country plantation life.

Beyond the dining room's Sheraton and Hepplewhite is one of the flanker rooms.

A flanker-wing study stands
 above the near azalea garden.

Mulberry's living-room furniture is mostly from the eighteenth century.

Along the Lower James

St. George Tucker, law professor, lived here in 1789.

The 1799 house of an early judge, James Semple.

Built about 1756, here actress Sarah Hallam died.

The reconstructed house of William Levingstone.

THERE are two distinct parts to the program of the Colonial concert that is played along the lower James. One is devoted to the harmonious symphony of town buildings known as Colonial Williamsburg; the other includes at least five separate masterworks—the beautiful country mansions called Carter's Grove and Westover, Shirley, Berkeley and Brandon. Taken all together, it is probably the finest performance of eighteenth-century architecture in the country.

Like most of the early great plantation houses of the Southern tidewater sections, these opulent dwellings were built where they could best be reached by boat, the land approaches then being little more than tracks through the wilderness. Indeed, this latter fact comes over you even today, as by long wooded ways you make your pilgrimage in spring to these grand old establishments. You get a feeling of what a trip it must have been to town for those first proprietors.

Town for them was Williamsburg, capital of the Colony of Virginia; and it was here that the wealthy owners of Westover, Carter's Grove and the rest came by boat and horseback to call on the governor at his palace, sit in the legislature, handle cases in court, and carry on their business affairs. Here they might meet up with George Washington for dinner at the Raleigh Tavern, take in a Congreve comedy with Thomas Jefferson, consult with Patrick Henry on a point of law, or discuss a son's college career at William and Mary with George Wythe, in the house which occupies the next two pages. Thanks to the munificence of Mr. Rockefeller, the town of Williamsburg has been so faithfully brought back to life that you see it now as it was two centuries ago. And here, on these pages, thanks to Mrs. Archibald McCrea, of Carter's Grove; to Mrs. Richard Crane, of Westover; and to the Colonial Williamsburg, we give you houses from both town and country at their best.

Westover

When William Byrd in 1729 wrote to a friend in London that "in a year or two I intend to set about building a very good house," he made something of an understatement; for what he did in fact erect was the masterpiece on the opposite page—the mansion called Westover. As you can see, the morning sun across the James lights up one of the loveliest façades in America, shines on one of the most beautiful doorways in the world.

Facing the Palace Green in Williamsburg is one of the purest examples of Georgian Colonial architecture in America.

The George Wythe House

The story goes that this beautiful house was built about 1755 by Richard Taliaferro for his daughter Elizabeth and her husband, George Wythe. Wythe was professor of law at the College of William and Mary, around the corner, where Thomas Jefferson had been a student. The latter, in fact, was a frequent visitor at the house, occupying it with his wife for a time in 1776 while the Wythes were in Philadelphia attending the Continental Congress. It was on that occasion that Wythe's pride in his home appeared rather gracefully in a letter to his distinguished guest: "The conveniency of my house and servants and furniture to you and Mrs. Jefferson adds not a little to their value in my estimation."

Still more historical luster is given the house by the fact that not only did Wythe entertain Washington there on the latter's early Williamsburg visits, but turned the house over to the great Revolutionary War general for use as his headquarters before the siege of near-by Yorktown.

Apart from the beauty of its architecture, the house as a home had the self-sufficiency of a huge plantation—on the scale, of course, of a town residence. On the grounds behind it there were gardens for flowers, vegetables, fruits; there were a stable, chicken house, lumber house, smokehouse, weaving house, laundry and kitchen—all separate small buildings in an orderly arrangement, and now all restored and completely equipped; the kitchen being the small frame building to the right of the main house in the photograph above.

It would appear from this that the Wythes lived well, and with cellars amply stored with food and drink, most of it grown right on the place; it is almost certain that they did. That they lived attractively, too, the pictures opposite prove.

One of the four beautiful bedrooms, furnished with pieces of the period.

Looking much as it did when Washington used to dine there.

The original paint colors of the study have been duplicated.

WESLEY BALZ—JOHN JOYCE, INC.

The carved staircase and main hallway, completely paneled in pine, are the climax of Carter's Grove's interiors, called the finest in America.

PRATT

Carter's Grove

This magnificent Colonial mansion, monumentally framed by enormous tulip poplars, faces out over the James from the topmost of its terraced lawns, six miles below Williamsburg. The downriver wing at the right was built in 1690; the upriver wing from five to ten years later; and the main central section between 1720 and 1730, when the English master builder, Richard Bayliss, was brought over to Virginia to design and carry out this most important part of the house, assisted by a fellow countryman, David Minitree.

*From the land side Carter's Grove still has the
plantation aspect—still functions as one.
Looming larger and larger as you approach it through
the fields, it rises beyond the lovely brick stables, growing
more and more beautiful the closer you come.*

Carter's Grove

It is typical of many Virginia mansions of the time that
Carter's Grove was built of materials that for the most part
were grown or manufactured right on the plantation. All the
timbers and framing were cut from forests on the property,
and all the famous paneling, of pine, walnut and poplar,
was carved from lumber off the place. Even the bricks
were baked on the site, of clay that was dug from the fields
which lay between the house and the river. What trans-
formed these local products into such a wonderful work of
art was the taste and intelligence of Carter Burwell, who
was proprietor of the plantation during the time that the
principal construction was done. His taste produced, no
doubt, the general idea, while his intelligence led him to
bring a builder like Bayliss from London for the design and

In the paneled drawing room, a duel was fought. One killed, one wounded.

execution. Burwell could hardly have done better, as Carter's Grove today bears beautiful witness, both inside and out.

However, not all the handwork on the house was performed by such a skillful craftsman. One bit of carving—on the stair rail in the main hall—is a vivid reminder of an incident that took place in 1781, when a Colonel Tarleton, in command of the British Light Horse Cavalry, was occupying Carter's Grove—his troops occupied in raiding the countryside. It seems that one night, in his cups, the colonel mounted his horse, rode into the hall and up the stairs, slashing at the rail with his sword on the way. The cuts have been carefully preserved, of course, and are carefully pointed out to visitors. The colonel's workmanship may be British, but it can't compare with his countryman's carving, though for the sake of the legend it is almost as precious.

This simply furnished and paneled room is called the office, and as such it is used, serving also as an informal sitting room and study. Its more primitive appearance is due to the fact that it occupies the up-river wing, built twenty-five years or more before the main part of the house.

In the delightful setting of this drawing room, George Washington is said to have proposed to a Williamsburg girl named Mary Cary, and Thomas Jefferson to Rebecca Burwell. Because of the nature of the response that was given there in both cases, it is now known as the Refusal Room.

43

From the entrance drive, Brandon composes beautifully into central body and symmetrical wings—the design, it is said, adapted by Thomas Jefferson from English architectural plates.

BRANDON

And across the James another Virginia masterpiece . . . Berkeley

BRANDON and Berkeley belong to that assembly of superb colonial mansions along the lower James, whose beauties were brought to your attention on the preceding eight pages with West-over, Carter's Grove, and the Wythe house at Williamsburg. All were built within a span of thirty years, beginning in 1726 with Berkeley and ending with Brandon, neither of which houses could ever have looked better than it does today. You might say the same of the neighborhood's whole pre-Revolutionary aspect.

Most of the houses, in a region whose fame in recent times has been revived by the restorations and reconstructions at Williamsburg, are in a sense hidden assets of this community; being off the beaten track and rarely open to the public. Brandon and Berkeley have never stopped keeping the plantation spirit alive. At Brandon, the present owner speaks with pride of the yield of corn; at Berkeley, they manage a magnificent herd of Herefords; life, though now in modern dress, goes on as ever. Washington, Jefferson and Patrick Henry no longer come over from Williamsburg as they did when it was a day's hard ride (now an easy hour by car); but the houses look essentially the same—just as elegantly reflecting the taste of their early days, which was something to celebrate, as you can see.

44

Through the doorway on the north side of Brandon's entrance hall you can see the spacious gardens leading to the James.

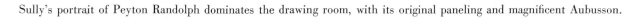

Sully's portrait of Peyton Randolph dominates the drawing room, with its original paneling and magnificent Aubusson.

PRATT

BERKELEY

JOHNSON

The river front is a fine example of the early Georgian fashion.

Both Berkeley and Brandon have had their ups and downs during their long lives, but now, their careers have been resumed in the manner to which they were first accustomed. Berkeley has been more recently restored than its distinguished neighbor at some distance across the river, and was more of an undertaking, the outside of the older house at some point having been covered with plaster; and while it had never been shelled from British gunboats on the James, as Brandon was, still bearing the scars on its garden porch, it had been served rather ruthlessly at times, and its splendid condition today is a tribute to its present owners, who have had the courage to treat it colorfully to fine effect. Both houses, being private homes, are open to the public only during Virginia's annual garden pilgrimage.

Handsome archways connect the north drawing room with its counterpart on the opposite page, together called the "Great Room." Barrel chair is Sheraton.

Portrait of Benjamin Harrison, the "Signer," and once owner, looks out on the old English silver, Hepplewhite chairs, Waterford glass and Chinese porcelain.

Aubusson rug and Louis XV settee add a French touch to this section of the "Great Room." Other pieces are Sheraton and Chippendale.

INTERIOR PHOTOS BY WESLEY BALZ-JOHN JOYCE, INC.

GUNSTON HALL

THE STORY OF FAMOUS OLD GUNSTON HALL, IN FAIRFAX COUNTY, VIRGINIA

JUST about the time George Washington was remodeling Mount Vernon for his marriage to Martha Custis, some friends of his, five miles down the Potomac, were moving into their brand-new house whose beauty today, while far less familiar to most of us than that of the first President's home, is still enough to take your breath away. Of course, when they walked into freshly finished Gunston Hall in the spring of 1758, the young George Masons were better prepared for the sight that met their eyes than anyone visiting the house for the first time now; they'd been watching it go up for a good three years. And it's practically certain that the general scheme of the house was pretty much George Mason's own; a knowledge of architecture then being part of any wealthy Virginian's possessions— along with plenty of money and slaves to put his notions into practice.

What Mason wanted in the way of a house, and what he got, as you can see, was a glorified Georgian cottage, much larger than it looks. Within the house, and without as well, he wanted the most wonderful woodwork to be seen in the Colonies, which in those talented times would take a lot of trying; but he succeeded in getting this too. The way he worked it was to send to London for a man named William Buckland, whose skill as a carver was unexcelled and whose knowledge of Classical ornament unsurpassed. Then Mason let Buckland loose with a simple Colonial plan to follow; gave him marvelous mellow white pine that would make your mouth water; hardwoods for framing which were seasoned to perfection; handmade over-size brick for the walls; limestone for the steps, foundations, corners—and hordes of help, falling all over themselves.

To this creation of that master craftsman and his perfectionist employer, time has now given a glow for which the Masons weren't able to wait. Life is too short. It must have seemed to them that the boxwood grew with tantalizing slowness; but

PHOTO BY PRATT

Across the parterred garden, laid out in the manner of the period by the present owner, the house rises above the age-old boxwood, a mansion of unusually modest appearance for a large manor house of the time.

PHOTO BY HAROLD FOWLER

Of the four main rooms on the first floor, the dining room is the simplest; at the same time, its figured blue paper makes it one of the most colorful. Notice the height of the cupboards as compared with the doorway.

PHOTOS BY FOWLER

Furniture makes no effort to compete with the glorious wood carving of the Palladian room, unequaled in this country; woodwork set off by the pine-paneled walls, no less effectively than when the pine was originally covered with what was probably a figured damask—the tack holes still visible.

Above the mantel in the library is fixed a facsimile of the Virginia Declaration of Rights, the historic document written by George Mason, the original owner of Gunston Hall, who was a close friend and neighbor of George Washington.

The view through the doorway leading from the Chinese Chippendale room to the hallway not only indicates the unusual, and unusually beautiful, woodwork decoration of the room, but the spaciousness and dignity of the big entrance hall beyond.

now, having had almost two centuries to attain its present monumental proportions, it has become the great feature of the grounds. And indoors, all this while, the passage of nearly two hundred years has given the woodwork an almost magical quality—or so it seems to eyes accustomed to the somber miracles of modern machinery. George Mason, whose body lies buried near the house, has given a glow himself to American history, as the author of the Virginia Declaration of Rights, the basis of our Constitution's Bill of Rights, and the major part of the Constitution of Virginia, and as a man whom Jefferson called the wisest of his generation. But when you walk into the drawing room of Gunston Hall, the brilliance you feel is Buckland. The handiwork of that inspired English carpenter is the light that lingers in your vision when you leave.

Listen briefly to the way I imagine he worked; it may add to the pleasure you get from his windows, doorways, cornices, mantels and porches. For here was a man with taste as well as talent in his fingers, plus a complete command of Classical ornament, which was then the dominating motif in all design. A piece of clear pine laid out upon his bench was like the keyboard of a piano under his hands. He could take his tools and carve out the equivalent of a Mozart sonata, except that the music he followed was the music of Palladio, Vitruvius and Chippendale, who composed in stone and wood. No workman remembered now carried with him a larger library of Renaissance engravings or a better collection of contemporary handbooks, and I think of them as resting on a shelf above his bench, and Buckland carefully wiping his hands before consulting their pages.

THESE books were the architects that sailed from England in the early days to guide the craftsmen here when it came to questions of style; and to these books can be traced all the characteristics of design which we now call Colonial

*Gunston
Hall
in
Virginia.*

or Georgian. In the hands of a man like Buckland, these books came to life; more wonderfully in certain ways at Gunston Hall than anywhere else I know, and most wonderfully there, in my opinion, in the Palladian room, or drawing room, and the demioctagonal porch on the garden side, with the Chinese Chippendale room competing for my preference. Purists among present-day traditional architects may be inclined to quarrel with some of Buckland's proportions—the window heights, the tallness of the cupboards; but to me these so-called disregardings of the rules are triumphs of individuality. They are what give Gunston Hall its extraordinary charm, vitality and distinction—qualities that should be seen face to face to be fully appreciated.

Anyone can go to Gunston Hall. It is the private residence now of Mr. Louis Hertle, to whom we are indebted for the privilege of photographing it for the pleasure of our readers. Mr. Hertle makes any interested and appreciative visitor feel welcome, and the walls of his library are lined with the autographed pictures of prominent people who have enjoyed his hospitality and friendship—from Franklin Roosevelt back to William Howard Taft. It was about the time that Mr. Hertle acquired Gunston Hall, restored it with great regard for its original aspect, and deeded it, as a monument to be preserved for posterity, to the Commonwealth of Virginia.

You cut in from Route 1, about fifteen miles below Alexandria, following a country road for several miles toward the east. You come to some simple gateposts, and a winding lane, and at the end of the lane you come to the house. If it is spring, and the dogwoods are in bloom, the house may seem to be standing in a soft, mysterious pool of light. But I have imagined this strange luminosity in midsummer, too, and in winter; so it may be merely the memory of Buckland. At any rate, you can't mistake the house. There is nothing quite like it anywhere else I know.

PHOTOS BY PRATT

The porch that faces the gardens is a partial octagon in shape, and probably the only original porch of its kind in the country; an outstanding example of William Buckland's skill as an adapter and designer from classical models; for there is a theory that this design was derived from an engraving of a Roman coin that shows a similar feature in the Temple of Tyche in Eumeniea. From it you get a beautiful view of the gardens and look down the allée shown opposite.

From one of the bedrooms on the second floor you look down across the ancient box-bordered allée that separates the two parterred gardens, and over the intervening landscape to the Potomac and the shores of Maryland beyond. These gardens are beautiful all the year round, but they are at their best in the early spring, when the dogwoods and tulips are out.

By far the most outstanding feature of the grounds at Gunston Hall is the boxwood which, although it grows almost imperceptibly, has now attained impressive proportions in the course of nearly two centuries. It is especially effective in this allée from the garden house, overlooking the view toward the river, and the porch that appears close-up at the left on this page.

ALEXANDRIA

TWO hundred years ago this summer, on a pleasant piece of land sloping down to the Potomac, a young man of sixteen, lugging one end of a surveyor's chain, was helping to lay out the site of a town to be named after a John Alexander, who in 1670 had bought the 6000 acres for 600 pounds of tobacco. Fifty years later, a few miles up the river, Congress was naming the new Capital of the United States after the former surveyor's assistant, who in the meanwhile had become famous as the Father of his Country. By that time, Alexandria had grown to be one of the most beautiful of the early American cities, and so it remains. For there are sections, like the two whole blocks of Prince Street at the right, which are still intact, with even the cobblestones as they were when they were laid by the Hessians just after the Revolution; and almost everywhere you turn in the older parts of town there is some handsome architecture to be seen.

These two blocks of Colonial and Federal houses on Prince Street have no equal

EXTERIOR PHOTOGRAPHS BY RICHARD PRATT-JOHNSON

HOLLAND
HOUSE

BUILT by a British sea captain in 1751, the present particular pride of this mellow old home down near the river is the dining room. The extraordinary table, set here for formal luncheon, is composed of four Chippendale tilt-top pedestals; the chairs, Chippendale; the hunting board, Hepplewhite. The table lace is *point de Venise;* the china, Queen Victoria's favorite pattern; the rug, a handsome Chinese replica. The setting and flower arrangements are by the owner, Mrs. Berenice Fleming-Holland.

nywhere for period completeness.

The drawing-room furniture is Sheraton; the chest and four-poster in the bedroom are American Chippendale.

INTERIOR PHOTOGRAPHS BY WESLEY BALZ-JOYCE, INC.

DULANEY HOUSE

THIS house was forty-one years old in 1824, when, on the occasion of a parade in his honor, the elderly but still debonair Marquis de Lafayette appeared at its doorway to address the throng and give a toast to the town. Within, as a labor of love, the richly carved interiors have been splendidly restored and preserved by its present owners, Mr. and Mrs. Howard Joynt, and furnished to perfection with the finest pieces of the period, making the house one of the choice examples of early American elegance in the United States.

SOUTHERN MARYLAND

EXTERIOR PHOTOGRAPHS BY RICHARD PRATT.   INTERIOR PHOTOGRAPHS BY BALZ-SELWYN LTD.

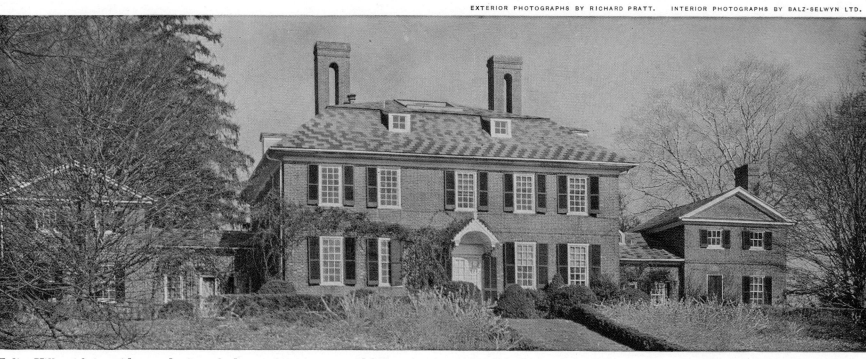

Tulip Hill, with its widespread wings, looks out from its terraced hilltop in Anne Arundel County over almost a mile of farmland to the Chesapeake Bay.

IT is true that in Annapolis, where Southern Maryland begins, there are more well-set-up midshipmen to make the place attractive than grace any other American city. But it happens that Annapolis, compared with any other American city, also contains more handsome Georgian houses of great distinction; and it is really because of this fact, beyond everything else, that the town is beautiful. Then for further beauty, from the neighborhood of Annapolis, where the Severn opens into the Chesapeake, all the way down to the Potomac, the back roads of Southern Maryland lead you to more fine Georgian plantations than can be found in any other region of equal size in the country. You can take, as two superb examples of what you will find, Whitehall, on the opposite page, whose portico faces out across the bay just before you come to Annapolis; and Tulip Hill, above, which is the first great house you discover after you leave. From there on, among the rolling hills and along the tidewater rivers, farther and farther away from the Naval Academy, the only competition the houses get comes from the landscape itself, which plays right into the picture.

Walking through Annapolis streets, you meet one masterpiece after another. The prize, in my opinion, is the Hammond-Harwood house, shown two pages farther on, the work of the same William Buckland who was the master carpenter of Virginia's famous Gunston Hall, pictured on page 48. Directly across the street, the stately Chase house, shown at the right below, and near by the Brice and the Paca houses, the latter now part of Carvel Hall, the former now made into apartments for many families where once one family lived in grandeur. Even the street names, like the streets themselves, carry you back to Colonial times: King George, Prince George, and the Duke of Gloucester Street, where the Ridout house, at the left below, stands out as a major masterpiece along a streetful of minor ones—the minor ones on many streets serving as a connecting chorus throughout the town to the cast of principals.

The Ridout house, in Annapolis, famous for the purity of its proportions.

The Chase house is one of the noblest and tallest of the Annapolis mansions.

Whitehall, near Annapolis, in Anne Arundel County, was built in 1765, and its Corinthian portico is one of the oldest in the country.

Near the crossroads village of Friendship at the lower tip of Anne Arundel County, Holly Hill's appearance is somewhat misleading, for with its single-story eaves it looks like a small house, which it isn't. Otherwise, there is nothing misleading about its looks, it being one of the loveliest and most appealing of Southern Maryland's old country houses, from its brickwork and windows and cornice right up to its chimneys.

HOLLY HILL

Being one of the earliest of the Georgian houses in Southern Maryland, Holly Hill has had plenty of time to acquire a history. One legendary fragment is that it was used by a pirate named Hogarth who had dug an underground passage to Herring Bay, half a mile away, through which he carried plunder from his boats. The place the "passage" enters the cellar can still be seen but, as the tunnel now extends only ten feet from the house, skeptics are inclined to doubt the story's authenticity. No one could possibly doubt, however, the authenticity of Holly Hill's age and beauty. Records show that the house was begun in the seventeenth century and finished early in the eighteenth, and it is obvious that its beauty was built into it. The marbleizing which covers the entire wood-paneled end of the main bedroom at the left, and the painting on wood above the fireplace are indications of its unusually charming interior, which was beautifully restored to its pristine condition about ten years ago by its present owners. Some of the original window-panes bear the diamond-scratched signatures of the early occupants of Holly Hill. But as yet no signature of the pirate Hogarth has been found.

HAMMOND-HARWOOD HOUSE

This has been called the most perfect example of Georgian architecture in America, and the chances are that that is a fairly safe estimate of its standing in the great community of Colonial houses which line the Eastern seaboard from Maine to Charleston. The charm and dignity of its design, along with its incomparable carving, are all the creation of the master carpenter, William Buckland, who was introduced to Annapolis by George Mason after Buckland had made such a success of Mason's Gunston Hall in Virginia. Its restoration and maintenance have been made possible by the proceeds from the annual pilgrimage which every spring makes most of the great old houses in Maryland accessible to the public.

Every detail of the Hammond-Harwood house, in Annapolis, is a work of art. The principal rooms in the main section of the house are all celebrated for Buckland's beautiful woodwork, but the dining room, with its carved shutters, is the showpiece.

KENNERSLEY . . . *Not far from the little town of Church Hill, in Queen Annes County, Kennersley dates from 1704, which was about a hundred years after the Eastern Shore was settled. This is the entrance front* *from the land; the water front faces out across the broads of the Chester River. The central section has fourteen-foot ceilings; the left wing is dining room, kitchen and servants' rooms, the right wing is for guests.*

EXTERIOR PHOTOGRAPHS BY PRATT; INTERIOR PHOTOGRAPHS BY BALZ—SELWYN, LTD.

THE ANCHORAGE . . . *This imposing mansion, viewed here from across the Miles River, near Easton, in Talbot County, was somewhat smaller and simpler in 1763, when it was purchased by the Reverend* *John Gordon, a pastor of St. Michael's parish, who was famous for the fact that behind his chapel down the river he ran a race track at which he and his congregation bet on one another's horses after services.*

THE EASTERN SHORE

A MAP of Maryland shows that the Eastern Shore of the Chesapeake has the crazily crooked edge of an uncompleted picture puzzle that someone has abandoned down the lefthand side in a mood of absolute defeat. It shows that this tangled scrollwork of coastline is caused by seventeen separate rivers cutting in, and by countless coves and inlets; but what the map can't show, of course, is the low-lying loveliness of all this intermingling land and water, and what wonderful settings it creates and keeps for some of the most beautiful old homes in America. It is as much as a map can do, in fact, to lead you to the houses, most of them having been built long before there were any roads, when people came and went entirely by water, whether it was Annapolis over the bay, or merely the next plantation. And with roads coming along so much later, as an afterthought, so to speak, you would naturally need a guide to find the hundreds of eighteenth-century houses worth seeing on the Eastern Shore. But fifty of the very best can be visited every spring on carefully planned explorations that uncover as well a hundred more great houses on the mainland of Maryland. For it is quite possible that this state as a whole contains more fine examples of Georgian Colonial than any other of the erstwhile colonies today, seen here and in the previous pages on Annapolis and the southern counties. . . . On the Eastern Shore, the far flat stretches of woods and fields which for the most part hide the old houses from the twentieth century are from year to year as unchanging as the views you get from the windows that face the water—down easy slopes and across the tides to farther shores. Safely tucked away in such locations, the houses that are still standing today have only a few familiar things to fear, like fire, neglect, mistreatment—harm from which, as you will see, the places shown here on these six pages have been most becomingly spared.

MYRTLE GROVE

Built in 1724

A writer recently said of Myrtle Grove that it "strikes a true balance between neglect and ostentation," which is a rather oblique way of describing its extraordinary charm and rare atmosphere—the result in part of its having remained in the appreciative possession of one family and their descendants from the time the first frame portion was built in 1724 until today. Inside and out it is one of the most naturally preserved of the famous old Eastern Shore houses. It stands on the banks of the Miles River, near Easton, in Talbot County, a few minutes' sail upstream from The Anchorage, which is just about ten times as far away by the roads that skirt the estuaries.

In the hallway of Myrtle Grove, with its beautiful doorway and cornice, hangs the portrait, by Charles Wilson Peale, of Judge Robert Goldsborough, his wife and two children, who were the occupants of the house when the brick section was added to the original part in 1790.

Among the choice features of the living room are the gold-and-white cornice boards topped by gilt eagles. And while you are casting your eyes on these, notice the finely modeled plaster cornice molding that surrounds the ceiling like a crown.

The dining room at Myrtle Grove is in the older frame section of the house, a room of chaste details and priceless heirloom furniture, with a portrait of an earlier Judge Goldsborough above the fireplace on the paneling of the chimney breast.

BOHEMIA

Built in 1745

Part of the unusual quality of glow and texture in Bohemia's façade is due to the all-header bond in which the bricks were laid, many of the bricks with glazed ends. This is a view from the land approach; the water front, as is typical, faces the river—in this case the Bohemia.

In addition to the unusual beauty of the whole mantel scheme from floor to ceiling in the living room of Bohemia, there is the unusual fact of its material, which is molded plaster. The Benjamin Franklin on the mantel is a Dresden figurine; in front an old celestial globe and Stiegel bottle.

The staircase at Bohemia is the spectacular feature of the house, no two panels of its Chinese Chippendale balustrade alike; the further architectural decorations of the rest of the hallway, above and below, being carried out in molded plaster; all in all, one of the sights of Cecil County. It was near the site of this house in Cecil County, by the way, that Augustine Herman settled to become one of the Eastern Shore's most important pioneers, a man from the province of Bohemia in what is now Czechoslovakia—which accounts for the name of the river, and this house as well.

THE READ HOUSE IN NEW CASTLE, DELAWARE, *could probably be called the showpiece of the town. That it is as fresh and fine today as it was when it was finished in 1801 is largely due to the tender care that has been given it by its present owners, Mr. and Mrs. Philip D. Laird. As with most important American houses of the period, and before, it follows the then prevailing popular English Georgian style.*

NEW CASTLE, DELAWARE

Distinguished

Colonial houses

of

old

New Castle.

A T least by Colonial reckoning, New Castle, Delaware, was already a rather old town in 1791 when George Read II, fifteen years after his father signed the Declaration of Independence, started to build this stately mansion with bricks brought down the river from Philadelphia by barge. The house took ten years to build, but it was time well spent, for when Read's master craftsmen finally laid down their tools, they had put up something for posterity.

Here on these two pages, for part of that posterity, is the way the Read house looks today, after being lived in for a hundred and forty-five years. And on the next two pages are glimpses of the town around it, where in early summer the Green, with its buildings of mellow brick, lies under the lavender canopy of tall paulownias, and the shady little streets are tightly set with house after handsome house, all still brightly reflecting a scene of centuries gone by. It is something not to miss.

Yet every year half a million motorists, passing by less than a minute away, miss it by barely a hundred yards. This is largely because the *new* town of New Castle has drawn a cordon of ordinary streets and ordinary houses around all but the river side of the old town; creating a kind of camouflage, through whose effect of ordinariness you unsuspectingly press on toward Florida or Maine. But whether you are heading north or south on this particular highway that brushes the skirts of New Castle, you are bound to pause at this point anyway, for it is here that you ferry the Delaware. And coming across the river from the New Jersey side, if you look a little off to the left, you can't help catching sight of the pink and white and yellow rows that front the old town; and then farther back above the roofs a sparkling white spire and two lofty white cupolas to give the place completely away—to anyone with his wits about him.

At any rate, the street you see from the river is called The Strand, and the most striking house you see along The Strand from the ferry is the Read house shown here. It's a good street to start on, and the Read house is one of the first you meet, with its elegant Georgian façade facing out across the river. But when you look farther up The Strand, if you're anything like me, the lure of the town has caught you, and you make up your mind to give a quick preliminary glance at everything, then come right back for a longer look—and at everything else, all over again. You think if it's all been there this long, it will certainly stay for another few minutes—though you yet aren't sure it's absolutely real (and that's not just a way of talking).

By the time you've hurried up the fairly long unbroken block of The Strand, with your eyes popping out, you've made the full front width of the old town. One long block wide, and three shorter blocks back from the river, contain everything you want to see. You come to a broad open street and see first the town hall and courthouse,

The great fanlight above the wide double doors, leading from the living room into the reception room, is a unique architectural feature of this famous house. The musical instrument is a harp guitar of the period, and in the oval frame is a picture of Robert E. Lee as a young Army officer. The mirror is Queen Anne.

In the upstairs hall you look out across the river through the Palladian window, the outside of which you see in the façade on the opposite page.

On the marvelous mantel, are Lowestoft urns. The Hepplewhite table by the window is flanked by a Hepplewhite and a Queen Anne chair.

The furnishings in the dining room were collected by the owners since they acquired the famous old house. Here the table is Duncan Phyfe, the chairs Chippendale and the sideboard Hepplewhite. The silver was made in London at the time the house was built. The scenic paper shows views of old New Castle.

S ALEM'S memories begin with the Puritans, who settled there just six years after the landing at Plymouth Rock. And as far as posterity is concerned at present, those memories come to a climax with The Scarlet Letter, which was written on Mall Street there in the late 1840's by a sad, shy Salem man who had recently lost his job as surveyor of the port in the local customs office. In between, as you will recall, there was witchcraft. And there were the fabulous years of sailing ships, when riches from every region of the earth were heaped on Salem wharves, and Salem homes reflected the wealth of Salem merchants. These homes reflected, too, the talents of a Salem young man, a woodcarver by trade, with an extraordinary aptitude for architecture, whose taste and skill account for most of the major beauty which meets the eye in Salem today. For while in his comparatively short lifetime Samuel McIntire couldn't possibly have executed all the fine homes which Salem once possessed, it can be said that for all the best work in the great Salem tradition he was certainly the inspiration. The two great men of Salem never met; their lives overlapped too little. McIntire began the Pingree house, which appears on pages 100 and 101, in 1804, the year Hawthorne was born; and seven years later McIntire died at fifty-four. All his life was lived, and all his work was done, within a few miles of his native city; and it is a credit to Salem that there, in the midst of so very much now which scarcely measures up to McIntire, some of the master's finest achievements are still tenderly preserved. And for all that remain, the most outstanding, in my opinion, are the two which follow.

PHOTOGRAPHS BY PRATT

One long block of Chestnut Street is lined on both sides by Salem's largest remaining cluster of homes for which McIntire was directly or indirectly responsible.

Because of these capacious, foursquare houses, beautifully designed in the fashion of the Federal period, Chestnut Street has been called the architecturally finest residential street in America.

The sudden sight of this house as you come around the corner of Federal Street in Salem is almost overwhelming; so
little are you prepared for such magnificence in the midst of the commonplace encroachments that crowd about it now.

THE PEIRCE NICHOLS HOUSE

BUILT IN 1782

SAMUEL McINTIRE was in his early twenties when he designed this house for a wealthy East India merchant of Salem, named Jerathmeel Peirce—a man who obviously could afford the best, and in this case got it. For this was just about the finest wooden house in America. Not only was it McIntire's design, but every important piece of carving was done by his own hands, from the original urns that capped the fence-posts to the doorways, cornices and the mantels within. Like most early American craftsmen, McIntire lacked any formal training in architecture; but as far as he was concerned, you could hardly call this a handicap. What simplified matters somewhat for him was an English volume of architectural details, very much in vogue over here since well before the Revolution, a book called The City and Country Builder's and Workman's Treasury of Designs, by a man named Batty Langley; and from it McIntire got many of the ornamental features which distinguish this extraordinarily handsome house, such as the Doric order of the façade and the Georgian mantel of the dining room at the right. But of course the main conception was McIntire's alone: the general mass and plan, and the bold idea of the great Greek corner pilasters that did so much, you can be sure, to please Mr. Peirce as he paced his balustraded roof deck, peering out across the bay for the tall sails of a clipper coming in from China.

When the house was built, the dining room at the right was
the drawing room, its carving in McIntire's early manner.

98

The east drawing room, with its exquisite carving in the Adam fashion, was finished by McIntire somewhat later than the one below, in time for the marriage of Sally Peirce to George Nichols. The teak tables were brought back from China as ballast.

PRATT

Few houses in America present façades of such effective symmetry. One of McIntire's last houses, its simplicity is noteworthy.

PINGREE HOUSE

BUILT IN 1804

THE spirit of Samuel McIntire must find profound satisfaction with the way this wonderful brick house of his has been preserved and the faithfulness with which it has been restored and furnished. It is a tribute not only to the craftsman who created it, but to the generosity and painstaking care of its present patrons and protectors; and I only wish that hundreds of other famous American houses might be so fortunate as this one. At any rate, here you can feel at first hand the taste of those early times when skillful craftsmen and prosperous clients worked together in such close accord with the image of England in mind. On the day of his death it was written that, *"This day Salem is deprived of one of the most ingenious men it had in it . . . indeed, all the improvements of Salem for nearly thirty years have been under his eye. He had a fine person, a majestic appearance, calm countenance, great self-command and amiable temper. He was welcome but never intruded."* And on his tombstone you can read, *"He was distinguished for Genius in Architecture, Sculpture, and Musick: Modest and Sweet Manners rendered him pleasing: Industry and Integrity respectable: He professed the Religion of Jesus in his entrance on manly life; and proved its excellence by virtuous Principles and unblemished conduct."* Few men, it must be said, lie buried beneath such a tribute to their character, or amid so many mementos of their taste and skill.

The bedroom below is within the two right-hand second-story windows, and its most impressive piece of furniture is of course its great Directoire bed with the studded leather chest at its foot. Above McIntire's mantel is a painting of Salem harbor.

FOWLER

Marvelously carved sliding doors separate the front and back parlors on the right of the main entrance. The wallpaper panels are French, the side chairs are the finest examples of Hepplewhite, the piano is by Benjamin Crehore, and the rug is an Aubusson.

The entrance hall leads past McIntire's handsome staircase balustrade, and under his archway to the garden door. The wallpaper is by the English carver, Grinling Gibbons.

The dining room, at the left of the entrance, is furnished in Sheraton, and the magnificent mahogany set off by superb pieces of silver.

The robin's-egg-blue bedroom is furnished in the French Chippendale style, showing Chinese influence, and typical Salem perfect taste.

WOODSTOCK, VERMONT

Some of the handsome old houses that add charm to the Woodstock Green.

The early Converse house, built of the beautiful Woodstock-made brick.

Wandering through Woodstock, the enchanted visitor comes to the conclusion that this old town, so clearly well to do, must thrive on its charm and beauty alone, for he looks in vain for any other visible means of support. That is to say, there are no railroads, and, as far as he can see, no factories; the air of the town consequently is clear and quiet, most appropriate to the period quality of the place, whose appealing old houses date from the early part of the past century, when Vermont was catching up architecturally with the rest of the young republic.

There was already a lot of local wealth in Woodstock back in 1786, when it became the county seat of Windsor County, for the marble and granite quarries of Vermont were being opened and Vermont gorges were being dammed for water power; and with the courts and county offices in Woodstock, the town drew in quite a few legal lights and prosperous operators. This, of course, accounts for the substantial character of Woodstock architecture from the start, while the quality of its design, which remained remarkably high until about a hundred years ago, and has been a good influence ever since, can be credited to the carpenter craftsmen who worked their way inland from places like Portsmouth and Boston, where they had learned their trade among a multitude of earlier American masterpieces.

Now, as you amble under the elms of the famous Green, and turn the corner at the end down Elm Street, the past comes pleasantly to life, and you feel it is in safe hands here forever.

Beyond the Johnson house, of 1809, on Elm Street, with its Ionic porch, you see the lovely tower of the Old White Meeting House.

THE LYMAN MOWER HOUSE

If this is Woodstock's most impressive house today, it must have seemed doubly so when Lyman Mower built it in 1823. Young Lyman picked a fitting location facing the Green for the elegant mansion he had in his mind, then gave the job to superlative workmen who drew on builders' handbooks of the day for the details of its design. There was wood to burn in Vermont, of course, but Mower had his heart set on brick, and brick the house became, of bricks made locally, whose beautiful tawny red color is seldom seen elsewhere. The style is a modified Georgian now known as Federal, and the great end walls, handsomely windowed and chimneyed, give the house an almost monumental appearance.

An episode in the history of the house is part of local lore, for when a native of the town, Frederick Billings, who had gone to California during the gold rush and found himself a multimillionaire almost overnight, heard that his parents had become impoverished and were in debtors' confinement back home, he returned at once and bought them this, the finest house in Woodstock.

It is still the finest, inside as well as out, it having had the good fortune to be acquired recently by Mr. Lee Anderson, who, though not a native of Woodstock, has feelingly restored and furnished it with the distinction it deserves, as you can see.

Lyman Mower in 1823 built himself a house for the ages.

Haydon's painting of young Victoria surveys the drawing room with its Kermanshah rug, satinwood desk, French chairs, and early pine cabinet in the corner.

The Chippendale chair and Chinese Chippendale desk are library features.   *Dining chairs are Hepplewhite; table, Sheraton; mirror, Chippendale.*

THE WARREN-KIDDER HOUSE

Above the Federal porch, a Palladian window and a scroll-topped dormer.

This house, around the corner from the Green, on Elm Street, was built in 1807 by Simon Warren, descendants of whom have occupied it ever since, through four generations, a record characteristic of Woodstock. It is of frame, with typical New England narrow clapboards, and a porch in the Federal style so popular when the house was put up. Certain fanciful touches, like the scroll of the central dormer and the variturned balusters of the staircase, give the impression that the carpenter craftsmen who worked on these features back in 1807 must have enjoyed their job. And the house has remained to give enjoyment to everyone who passes it and has a chance to look inside; for within, quite apart from the staircase that marches up in three-tone chords, every room contains distinguished pieces of fine old furniture, much of it having been handed down from one generation of the family to the next through the long history of the house.

Sheraton four-poster with oval-topped canopy.

The banquet table will expand from four-person to sixteen-person size.

ANDALUSIA

THE GREEK REVIVAL AT ITS BEST

BACK in the early part of the last century, Greece was fighting for her life against the Turks; and so frenzied were the feelings here in her behalf that there was talk of organizing private armies to help her, and towns from Maine to Florida were taking Attic names like Alpha, Athens, Euclid, Delta, Sparta, Troy and Ypsilanti. And houses all the way to the Mississippi began to look more or less like temples of the gods, creating a fashion that carried right up to the fifties, with results that ran from almost sublime to nearly ridiculous—a fashion now known as the Greek Revival. You must have seen at least some of its houses, with their serious Classic porticos, their columns and pilasters; and if you are at all familiar with the 1830 towns of Western New York, Northern Ohio and Southern Michigan, you

must have seen quite a few. But unless you have been fortunate enough to have seen Andalusia, you have missed the most important dwelling of the period. So here it is.

The broad lawns of Andalusia sweep down to the Delaware not far up the river from Philadelphia, with hardly anything to meet the eye that wouldn't have met it in the 1830's. And looking up from the river bank, you see what appears to be the Temple of Poseidon, translated into wood from the famous remains left by the Greeks at Paestum, now pillowed against Pennsylvania trees, and giving Classic grandeur to a fine old Pennsylvania mansion whose rooms live up in every way to the promise of that splendid portico. But before we look inside, let me tell you how it happened.

EXTERIOR PHOTOGRAPHS BY RICHARD PRATT   INTERIOR PHOTOGRAPHS BY BALZ-SELWYN LTD.

Looking up at a corner of the great Doric portico at Andalusia, its painted woodwork feels absolutely right as the face for this large and livable mansion.

One of the two yellow drawing rooms at Andalusia, glowing with gilt and decorated with Greek details of the period on overmantel and the surrounding cornice.

Looking from one yellow drawing room to the other, you see on the right a portrait of Nicholas Biddle, who, as Andalusia's owner, was largely responsible for Greek Revival in America.

The marble mantel of the music room was imported from Italy; most of the Empire furniture came from France, at that time under the influence of Classic forms.

For the story of Andalusia is the story of a style that was started, if by any one man, by Andalusia's owner at the time—a man named Nicholas Biddle.

For years the nation's leading financier, a statesman of note, scholar, editor, connoisseur, Biddle was constantly in the news. He was one of our earliest travelers to Greece, and his thrill for the wonders of her ancient architecture turned out to be amazingly contagious here, for as a prominent public figure his words would carry far and wide, and people listened. Then, too, this country's sympathies for Greece were being whipped up by Byron's poems on that nation's plight, and in addition we identified our recent struggles for liberty with the fight that Greece was making then for independence. But what really turned all this intense concern into an urge to get Greek feeling into our houses was the timely appearance of the first measured drawings ever made of the fabulous

monuments on the Acropolis, together with handbooks from England which adapted those drawings to practical use. And with all these data, and all that public desire, you can be sure our builders and architects wasted no time in getting to work.

And you can be sure that in putting his own architect to work on Andalusia, it was Nicholas Biddle who supplied the inspiration for one of the first and certainly most famous examples of a style that was soon to sweep the East and even what was then the West.

The architect he chose was Thomas U. Walter, of Philadelphia, one of the designers of the Capitol at Washington, and the work that Walter did was in the nature of an addition to the forty-year-old Regency house built by Biddle's father-in-law, John Craig. But the result, at least from the river side, was a complete transformation from Regency to a bold and brooding Doric edifice, which in spite of its cool classicism

The portico of Andalusia looms up from the lawn like the temple from which it was copied.

The dining room of Andalusia is in the older Regency section of the house, but its decoration and most of its furniture discreetly place it in the subsequent period of the famous Greek Revival addition. On the marvelously polished mahogany Empire table is an arrangement of horse-chestnut blossoms and branches.

had extraordinary warmth, and in spite of its immense proportions, had really livable scale.

There were to be even more ambitious achievements than Andalusia in the way of Classic emulation, of which Berry Hill, in Virginia, is an outstanding example, it being completely surrounded by columns, like the Parthenon.

But strangely enough, the temple effect in almost every house that followed Andalusia took on a residential quality; quite dignified, of course, in many cases, but amazingly homelike, considering the fact that the original temples were never designed for living. Leave it to the ingenuity of American carpenters and architects of the time to have made the transformation, though they could hardly have helped it if they were going to reduce the proportions to fit plain people, use wood instead

of stone, and provide regular doors and windows, along with chimneys, downspouts and all the other domestic devices. And as you have probably noticed, most of our Greek Revival houses are far less pure in style than Andalusia, which bears a remarkable resemblance to the original temple that Biddle chose to adapt. The liberties which carpenters took with the Greek details in a great majority of cases often produced a noteworthy naïveté and romantic charm—produced, in fact, a style that was eminently American, just as English Georgian had earlier, in this country, become Colonial.

The liberties taken grew greater as the Greek Revival went on, with more and more results that now seem rather quaint and amusing; until finally, in the fifties, people's preoccupation with Classic forms gave way entirely to the craze for Gothic. But that is quite another story.

The great garden of Andalusia, with its flowing trees, lies between two high walls, draped with wistaria.

The bookcases, painted with Classic decoration of the period, and the elegant old fruit-wood sofa, are features of the Biddle library at Andalusia.

GREEN LEAVES

D'EVEREUX

NATCHEZ

Where the fragrance of ante-bellum splendor is kept forever fresh

114

DUNLEITH

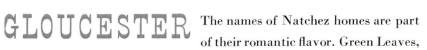

The small library at Gloucester has an eighteenth-century mantel from France, Meissen garnitures from Germany, a secretary from England and paintings from Italy—typical of the importations of the time.

GLOUCESTER

The names of Natchez homes are part of their romantic flavor. Green Leaves, D'Evereux and Dunleith; Gloucester, Monteigne, Monmouth and Arlington; Longwood, Lansdowne, Linden, Rosalie, Hope Farm, Stanton Hall and Elgin; Richmond, Airlie, Mistletoe, and on and on: names and houses ornamenting the old town that stands high above the brown Mississippi and decorating the lush surrounding countryside. Gloucester is a good beginning, for it was the home of the first territorial governor, a rigid New Englander, named Winthrop Sargent, who came to this already colorful community about 1800, tried his Yankee best to resist its blandishments, and finally gave in to its luxurious delights. He now lies buried beneath a great magnolia on the lawn of his house whose Georgian manner he might have brought with him from Massachusetts—a style that the climate of Natchez embellished after its own exuberant fashion.

The upholstered pieces in the yellow drawing room at Gloucester show the effect of the Victorian fashion which found the Natchez homes such willing and wonderful settings for its romantic elegance.

The guest bedroom at Monteigne is dominated by its chinoiserie chintz; its great tester bed and rosewood chairs in the best imported Victorian taste of the times.

MONTEIGNE

Younger than most of the Natchez homes, Monteigne was scarcely ten years old when Union soldiers were stabling their horses in its drawing rooms. But it survived this Civil War vandalism, and its condition today, as you can see, is practically perfect, its classic portico rising as proudly as ever before its beautifully proportioned pink façade. Set against a background of enormous live oaks, Monteigne is surrounded by great gardens of roses, camellias and azaleas, the soft night air heavy with their sweet smells and the daytime brilliant with their blossoms. In point of time, Monteigne marks the close of the golden age of Natchez, much as Hope Farm and Gloucester marked its beginning. From the end of the eighteenth century to the start of the Civil War, the Natchez district was peopled with families of fabulous wealth who loved to live elegantly. The ships which carried their cotton to the Eastern seaboard, to England and the Continent, carried them, too, and brought them back with the finest of furnishings for their homes and with the most cosmopolitan ideas for an idyllic life in this faraway community.

Generations of hand polishing have produced a rich patina on the fine eighteenth-century furniture of the Monteigne dining room, where the light glitters on lavishly scaled repoussé silver and a delicate Venetian chandelier. Especially fine is the pair of Sevres vases on the mantel.

Monteigne's entrance hall, with its marble floor, its harplike balustrade and its hand-blocked French scenic wallpaper, is one of the most stunning eye-catchers in the whole stunning Natchez neighborhood.

In keeping with the scale of the house, the double drawing rooms of Stanton Hall open into a ballroom seventy-two feet long, whose full length you can see reflected in the immense gilt-framed mirror at the end, glittering with the light of the massive bronze French chandeliers.

STANTON HALL It was typical of the flush times in Natchez in 1851 that the builder of Stanton Hall should have chartered a whole ship to bring from Europe materials and furnishings for his new home—not to mention further importations from abroad which were required during the five years before the house was finished. As handsome as are the solid-silver hinges, knobs and key plates that came from England for the doors, the lacy iron grillwork that came by the ton from Italy for the porches is handsomer still. And indoors no expense was spared on the carved white Carrara marble mantels or on the bronze French chandeliers that hang from ceilings more than twenty-two feet high. There is no record of Stanton Hall's original cost, but as a sign of fallen grandeur it was sold during the boll-weevil depression for $9700. Since then it has been bought by one of the Natchez garden clubs as headquarters for its annual tours of the famous old homes, and also serves as a rather fabulous guesthouse.

HOPE FARM
The oldest of the grand-manner homes of the Natchez district, Hope Farm dates from the days of the Spanish occupation. It is really two separate houses, joined by galleries, the older and larger built in 1775, and the smaller in 1789 by Don Carlos de Grandpré, a French adventurer who was a governor of the district during the Spanish regime. Its design is simpler, its ceilings lower, than those of the houses that went up when the United States took over the territory, but the care with which it has been restored makes it one of the most charming in the Natchez district.

The furnishings of Hope Farm show many influences, from the early Federal furniture of the dining room above, through the nineteenth-century bedsteads, chairs and dresser of the bedroom at the bottom of the page, to the elegant Victorian pieces of the cool inside parlor just below.

GREEN LEAVES The twin parlors of Green Leaves, of which the room above is one, are identical except for details in their priceless accessories. The Beltzhoover family makes everyday use of both rooms, amid the Meissen and Sevres, the Watteau fans, the ivory miniatures, rare prints and manuscripts, and autographed albums of Confederate generals and other memorabilia of the War Between the States. And in the game room at the left it is as though time had stood completely still for a hundred years or more.

ARLINGTON More than a century ago the library at Arlington *(left above)* was filled with eight thousand rare volumes, purchased in London, meticulously cared for ever since on the shelves that surround the room, whose tremendous scale is given away by the armchair in the corner. In the room at right, the present owner of Arlington keeps her famous collection of glass, the shelves having been effectively set against the windows of the gallery to bring out the beauty of old Bristol, Bohemian, Waterford and English crystal.

THE ELMS The back parlor at The Elms still has its original Victorian furniture intact, still upholstered in the now-seldom-seen original Windsor patterns. Also seldom seen nowadays are such items as the lily sconces above the mantel and the graceful rosewood escritoire. The bell pull beside the window rings its specially toned bell in the pantry, where each room has its own bell.

LINDEN Most Natchez homes had punkahs, or breeze fans, in their dining rooms, swung gently back and forth with strings by colored boys during the midday dinner, which is still the principal meal in Natchez homes.

LANSDOWNE The drawing room at Lansdowne represents the nineteenth century at its most fabulous, with a double set of rosewood furniture from France still covered in its original brocade. Imported at the same time as the furniture were the hand-painted wallpaper, the carpet, cornices and brocatels, making in all one of the most remarkable rooms of its period in the country.

VIEUX CARRÉ . . . *The streets in the old quarter have names like Iberville, Toulouse, Bienville, Bourbon, Dumaine and Chartres; and as you walk along under the lacy galleries you hear snatches of Creole French, and look through dark passageways into patios filled with sunlight and palms. Off the end of the street ahead, the Cathedral of St. Louis flanks a luxuriant square; and a few steps farther on oysters Rockefeller and the trout Marguery are as out-of-this-world as the Quarter itself.*

EXTERIOR PHOTOGRAPHS BY RICHARD PRATT; INTERIOR PHOTOGRAPHS BY HENRY FLANNERY

BLANC HOUSE . . . *Northwest of the Quarter, along Bayou St. John, are some of the early West Indian plantation houses, of which this is by far the most striking.*

BUCK HOUSE . . . *The symmetry and generous proportions of Garden District houses make an effective foil for their costumes of color and shadow.*

NEW ORLEANS

YOU can see what Thackeray and Mark Twain meant when they called this a Paris in America—which it isn't exactly; but the flavor of the famous old Creole Quarter is decidedly French provincial; and for a flavor of another sort you encounter in farther parts of the city occasional countrylike plantation houses that are marvelous in the moonlight; while in what they call the Garden District, where the air is scented with sweet olive blossoms, and the houses give off an aroma of antebellum elegance in settings of almost tropical lushness, you find still another flavor, that could be called crinoline. Altogether, it makes a unique and romantic potpourri, French, Spanish, English, named New Orleans. With the accent on the *Or*.

123

ROBINSON HOUSE . . . *In the Garden District, as well as the Quarter, many houses decorate themselves with delicate ironwork like lacy overlays for a valentine.*

PIRATE'S ALLEY . . . *Like a little street in the south of France. Notice that French Quarter façades may be repaired, but never modernized.*

THE COURTYARD *of the Gauche house tinkles with the splash of the tall fountain, and the air that rustles the big banana leaves is fragrant with flowers. A gallery above connects the main house and the guests' and servants' quarters.*

The shutters, ordinarily closed for coolness and quiet, were opened as a favor for this photograph.

THE
GAUCHE HOUSE
IN THE VIEUX CARRÉ

Iɴ the days when the Vieux Carré was almost exclusively Creole, and the Old Quarter was the special domain of the haughty French-Spanish set, John Gauche built this house at Esplanade and Royal, and hung its simple foursquare outside walls with cornices and galleries lined with lacy ironwork. The tallness of the windows gives away the wonderful ceiling heights within, upstairs and down. And inside, the present owner has given her rooms the French elegance they must have enjoyed at the hands of John Gauche in the Fifties, when only French furnishings were considered suitable for Creole homes.

THE DRAWING ROOM *here is one of two on the first floor, which further contains the immense dining room and the large study of the owner, Miss Mathilda Gray, who says that her house takes a party for six or six hundred, at will.*

THE BEDROOM *of the owner recalls the splendor not only of earlier Creole days in New Orleans, but of the old haut monde of France itself, for much of the furniture here was brought by Miss Gray from her country house near Paris.*

In the old days the main central part of the house was the domain of the parents and daughters; the wings were the garçonnière, or quarters for the sons of the family and for the steady stream of guests who came by horse and carriage from the city and from plantations surrounding the countryside.

ORMOND

PLANTATION

A FEW miles up the Mississippi River from New Orleans in a wide sweeping bend of the river, this plantation house, as you approach it from the road below the levee, appears very much as it must have looked when it went up, although the brick wings were added later. Built by the Butler family in the 1780's, its wide galleries clearly show a Spanish influence; its columns are typical of Louisiana.

THE LOWER HALL *leads from the entrance through a broad archway into a kind of casual sitting room that in turn leads out upon a garden stretching off into the distance between two great rows of camellias.*

STRACHAN HOUSE

This handsomely porticoed home in the Garden District is the house where Jefferson Davis died. Ionic below and Corinthian above, the columns of this double gallery create an architectural effect familiar in the neighborhood, while indoors the woodwork and furnishings are notable, even for New Orleans.

HURST PLANTATION
A house that was moved to the new residential district from the banks of the Mississippi, five miles away. After its journey this fine old plantation house was given a setting its tradition and beauty deserved. An extraordinary Coromandel screen dominates the drawing room.

THIS beautiful adobe church was built in the 1790's at near-by Carmel. The work was done by native Indian labor under the skillful direction of Manuel Estévan Ruiz, a master mason from Spain. The heavy tile roof held until 1852, when along with the fortunes of Monterey it collapsed—many of the tiles being taken to patch the roofs of that temporarily forsaken town. Now carefully restored, its patio splendidly gardened, it is the showpiece of the peninsula.

Monterey

Where Spain and New England combined in creating a style that has since spread all over the country

Once in the center of the city, the charming Casa Bonifacio has been reconstructed with its original adobe in the more congenial setting of an open residential section.

In the ancient but beautifully preserved customhouse, close to famous Fisherman's Wharf, ship arrivals in the old Spanish and Mexican days were celebrated with revels.

WINDING through the town of Monterey, there runs a continuous orange-yellow strip, painted down the center of certain streets like a traffic line; a slender golden track, with arrows urging you to follow the trail. If you do, you come in the course of your little trip to every old house of any distinction in the city; each house marked by an attractive plaque like the one for the De la Torre adobe at the bottom of this page. But because along the route each indicated house is in itself also marked by special qualities which alone are enough to capture the attention, the signs are simply footnotes to the story that unfolds as you trace out the line.

The story of the houses begins with the time when California was a colony of Spain, and Monterey the most important seaport on the coast. Timber was plentiful, but lumbermen and carpenters weren't; and besides, the Indians already had a building material that was better and easier by far. They merely molded blocks of mud from the ground, let them dry hard in the sun, and laid them up into walls—a trick that had worked its way up from Mexico, where adobe had been a building material for thousands of years. And with the simple plastered stone-walled houses of their native Mediterranean in mind, the Spaniards then had at hand a manner, as well as a method, of building which made a heavenly marriage in the climate of Monterey, creating a tradition which of course the Mexicans carried on when eventually they took over from the Spaniards.

In the meanwhile, as many of the Monterey houses make clear, Americans had been coming in, mostly from New England; and in the ships they sailed around Cape Horn, they carried not only certain architectural ideas from New England, but actual house parts too—doors, windows, moldings—along with Eastern carpenters who did their work the Eastern way. However, the basic form for Monterey houses had been established; adobe was ideal for the walls; the flat-pitched roofs with wide overhangs to shade the windows below were perfect for the climate; so these important characteristic features were retained. It is only in the woodwork that the houses tell their Eastern inheritance; but the blending of the two Colonials was such a happy one that the style created here has after a hundred years become the most popular in the country, next, of course, to the Cape Cod cottage—which, after all, was one of its forebears.

Some of the houses still show what happened to Monterey in the 1850's, shortly after California became part of the United States. Gold had been discovered—but just too far away. The town became deserted, and the houses for many years were left at the mercy of the weather. But there is a happy ending, as you can see, for practically all those which remain have been beautifully restored—and the others make most romantic ruins.

Half-hidden here under flowering trees, the De la Torre house, one of Monterey's most appealing adobes, was once sold, during the hard times, for $7.50 in back taxes.

EXTERIOR PHOTOGRAPHS BY RICHARD PRATT

INTERIOR PHOTOGRAPHS BY HENRY FLANNERY

A FEW years after he came to Monterey from Boston in 1832 and built this house, Thomas Oliver Larkin, who by then was already one of the first citizens of California, furthered a style which, in bringing together Eastern Colonial and Spanish Provincial, has become traditional with Monterey. Characteristic features: long horizontal lines, hip roof, porches.

DOMINATED by the huge, intricately carved teakwood Chinese bed, and further set with other Chinese pieces, paintings and accessories, the principal bedroom of the Larkin house shows the influence that is naturally reflected in a home so closely associated with trade between California and the Orient. Note the pioneer simplicity of the plank ceiling.

THE deep embrasured windows of the Larkin house dining room reveal the thickness of walls laid up of large sun-dried adobe bricks, plastered and whitewashed; while the furniture from early New England completes the picture of the life of the first wealthy settlers from the East who did so much to develop Monterey's now familiar architectural manner.

The Larkin House

THE garden of the Casa Amesti, one of the loveliest adobes in Monterey, is a tribute to the taste of its present owner, the well-known decorator, Frances Elkins, who has not only restored the fine old house with great sensitivity but has embellished it inside and out in a manner that equips it most appropriately for contemporary living. The garden has a distinctly Mediterranean flavor, the formality of the clipped boxwood and columnar yews relieved by the softer forms of lemons and fig trees and palms.

The Amesti House

MRS. ELKINS' little blue library reflects, as it should, the personality of the present owner of the old Amesti house, just as the cool old thick-walled building itself still very much emanates its original atmosphere of simplicity. It was built in the 1830's by a rich ranchero of the region, Don José Amesti, who then a little later gave it to his daughter Carmen when she married Don Santiago (born James) McKinley, a former Scotch sailor who was left ashore off a whaler at San Francisco in the '20's and became a naturalized Mexican—which would indicate that the house has romantic memories along with its architectural charm.

131

VISITING HISTORIC HOMES
SOURCES OF INFORMATION

HUNDREDS of our finest old American houses survive today through the active interest in and devotion to their preservation by local or regional organizations, many of which are listed below. Their assistance in providing information, in helping to secure permission to photograph, and in lending an able hand wherever necessary, leaves all of us involved in the preparation of this book deeply in their debt.

The following list may be helpful to anyone who is interested in visiting the areas covered in this book. These regions are listed with corresponding historical societies that have the latest information on tours, on which houses are open to the public, on entrance fees, dates, and hours of admission. New pamphlets and guidebooks are issued each year by most of these societies for the convenience of visitors.

ALEXANDRIA, VIRGINIA:
Alexandria Association, c/o Chamber of Commerce.

BUCKS COUNTY, PENNSYLVANIA:
Bucks County Historical Society, Doylestown, Pa.

CHARLESTOWN, SOUTH CAROLINA:
Historic Charlestown Foundation, 135 Church St.
Carolina Art Association, Gibbs Art Gallery.

CHARLOTTESVILLE, VIRGINIA:
Charlottesville Chamber of Commerce.
Thomas Jefferson Memorial Foundation (Monticello).
Garden Club of Virginia, Hotel Jefferson, Richmond, Va.

EASTERN SHORE, MARYLAND:
Hq., Federated Garden Clubs, The Belvedere, Baltimore, Md.
Maryland Historical Society, Baltimore, Md.
Hammond-Harwood House Assn., Annapolis, Md.

FAIRMOUNT PARK, PHILADELPHIA:
Fairmount Park Commission, c/o Museum of Art, Philadelphia, Pa.

GUNSTON HALL, VIRGINIA:
Garden Club of Virginia, Hotel Jefferson, Richmond, Va.

IPSWICH, MASSACHUSETTS:
Ipswich Historical Society (Whipple House and others).
Society for Preservation of New England Antiquities,

141 Cambridge St., Boston, Mass. (Emerson House and others).

JAMES RIVER HOUSES, VIRGINIA:
Garden Club of Virginia, Hotel Jefferson, Richmond, Va.
Colonial Williamsburg, Williamsburg, Va. (Wythe House and others).

LITCHFIELD, CONNECTICUT:
Litchfield Historical Society (Tapping Reeve House).

MONTEREY, CALIFORNIA:
Monterey Chamber of Commerce
State Division of Parks, Monterey (for Custom House).

NATCHEZ, MISSISSIPPI:
Pilgrimage Garden Club.
The Natchez Garden Club.

NEW CASTLE, DELAWARE:
New Castle Historical Society.
Delaware Society for Preservation of Antiquities.

NEW ORLEANS, LOUISIANA.
Chamber of Commerce.
Society for Preservation of Historic Centers.

PORTSMOUTH, NEW HAMPSHIRE:
Chamber of Commerce.
Portsmouth Historical Society (John Paul Jones house and others).
New Hampshire Society of Colonial Dames (Moffatt-Ladd House).
Society for the Preservation of New England Antiquities, 141 Cambridge Street, Boston, Mass. (Gov. Langdon House).

SALEM, MASSACHUSETTS:
Essex Institute (Peirce-Nichols and Pingree houses).

SOUTHERN MARYLAND:
Hq., Federated Garden Clubs, The Belvedere, Baltimore, Md.
Maryland Historical Society, Baltimore, Md.

ACKNOWLEDGMENTS

ALEXANDRIA:
Mr. Edward C. Van Devanter
Mr. James S. Douglas
Mr. and Mrs. Howard Joynt
Mrs. Berenice Fleming-Holland

ANDALUSIA: Mr. Charles J. Biddle

BUCKS COUNTY:
Mr. and Mrs. Charles T. Coiner
Mr. J. Carroll Molloy
Mr. J. Carroll Molloy, Jr.

CHARLESTON
Mr. Henry P. Staats
Mrs. H. J. Slocum
Mr. L. A. Walker, Jr.
Mr. Robert N. S. Whitelaw
Miss Helen G. McCormack
Mrs. Benjamin R. Kittredge
Mr. Herbert R. Sass
Mr. Pelzer Barry

CHARLOTTESVILLE:
Mr. Fiske Kimball
Mr. Winston Taliaferro
Mrs. Louis C. Martin
Mrs. Forney Johnson
Mr. Robert Hill Carter

EASTERN SHORE, MD.: Mrs. Blanchard Randall, Jr.
Mrs. H. Rowland Clapp
Mrs. Robert G. Henry

FAIRFIELD, CONN.: Miss Mary Allis

FAIRMOUNT PARK:
Mr. Fiske Kimball
Miss Sarah D. Lowrie
Mr. John P. B. Sinkler

GUNSTON HALL:
Mr. Louis Hertle
Miss Jessie M. Bishop

IPSWICH:
Mrs. Lovell Thompson
Prof. Langdon Warner
Mr. & Mrs. Robert G. Dodge
Mr. R. L. Bulger
Mrs. R. E. Ladd

JAMES RIVER:
Mrs. Richard Crane
Mrs. Archibald McCrea
Mrs. Douglas S. Freeman
Mrs. Robert W. Daniel
Mr. and Mrs. Malcolm Jamieson
Mrs. J. A. Johnston
Mr. B. W. Norton
Mr. A. Lawrence Kocher
Mr. James L. Cogar

LITCHFIELD:
Mr. Samuel H. Fisher
Miss Margaret Sanford
Mr. Robert Wright

MONTEREY:
Mrs. Alice Larkin Toulmen
Mrs. Frances Elkins
Mr. D. R. Jeffers

NATCHEZ:
Mrs. Theodora B. Marshall
Mrs. Mary Louise Giles
Mrs. Lenox Stanton
Mr. Thomas J. Reed
Mr. Earl Hart Miller

NEW CASTLE:
Mr. Philip D. Laird
Mr. Thomas Holcomb
Mr. Nicholas McIntire

NEW ORLEANS:
Mr. Marc Antony
Mrs. Mathilda Gray
Mr. E. A. Puderer
Mr. Clayton Fritchey
Mrs. Frank Strachan
Mr. Richard Koch
Mr. L. M. Williams

PORTSMOUTH:
Gov. Charles M. Dale
Miss Dorothy Vaughan
Mr. Bertram K. Little
Mrs. Wallis Walker
Mrs. William Kremer
Mr. and Mrs. Richman Margeson
Mr. W. G. Wendell
Mr. Ralph May

SALEM:
Mr. Russell Leigh Jackson
Mr. Ralph Lawson
Mr. John Carolyn

SANDWICH:
Mrs. Peter Place Cook
Mrs. Charles D. Cook
Mrs. Alice Evelyn Harvey

SOUTHERN MARYLAND: Mrs. Blanchard Randall, Jr.
Mrs. H. Rowland Clapp
Mrs. Lawrence Wharton
Mrs. Hugh P. LeClair
Mrs. Howard C. Davidson

WOODSTOCK:
Mr. Lee Anderson
Mr. and Mrs. Aubrey Lightbourn

BIBLIOGRAPHY

BENNETT, G. F.: *Early Architecture of Delaware*, Historical Press, Inc., Wilmington, 1932.

BRIGGS, M. S.: *The Homes of the Pilgrim Fathers in England and America*, Oxford University Press, New York, 1932.

COUSINS, F., and RILEY, P. M.: *The Colonial Architecture of Salem*, Little, Brown & Company, Boston, 1919.

DAVIS, DORSEY and HALL: *Alexandria Houses*, Architectural Book Publishing Company, Inc., New York, 1946.

EBERLEIN, H. D., and HUBBARD, C. V.: *Portrait of a Colonial City*, J. B. Lippincott Company, Philadelphia, 1939.

FORMAN, HENRY CHANDLEE: *Early Manor and Plantation Houses of Maryland*, Waverley Press, Baltimore, 1934.

FRARY, I. T.: *Thomas Jefferson, Architect and Builder*, Garrett & Massie, Inc., Richmond, 1931.

HAMLIN, TALBOT: *Greek Revival Architecture in America*, Oxford University Press, New York, 1944.

HANNAFORD, D. R., and EDWARDS, R.: *Spanish Colonial or Adobe Architecture of California*, Architectural Book Publishing Company, New York, 1931.

HIGGINS-WOOTEN: *New Castle, Delaware*, Houghton Mifflin Company, Boston, 1939.

HOWELLS, JOHN MEAD: *The Architectural Heritage of the Piscataqua*, Architectural Book Publishing Company, New York, 1937.

KELLY, J. FREDERICK: *The Early Domestic Architecture of Connecticut*, Yale University Press, New Haven, 1924.

KIMBALL, FISKE: *Domestic Architecture of the American Colonies and of the Early Republic*, Bobbs-Merrill Company, New York, 1928.

————: *Thomas Jefferson, Architect; Original Designs in the Collection of Thomas Jefferson Coolidge*, Riverside Press, Boston, 1916.

————: *Samuel McIntire, Carver, the Architect of Salem*, Southworth-Anthoensen Press, Portland, 1940.

MAJOR, HOWARD: *The Domestic Architecture of the Early American Republic: The Greek Revival*, J. B. Lippincott Company, Philadelphia, 1926.

RICCIUTI, ITALO W.: *New Orleans and its Environs*, William Helburn, Inc., New York, 1938.

STONEY, SAMUEL G.: *Plantations of the Carolina Low Country*, Carolina Art Association, Charleston, 1938.

WATERMAN, THOMAS T.: *The Mansions of Virginia*, University of North Carolina Press, Chapel Hill, 1945.

American Guide Series: Detailed guidebooks for all states represented in this book, prepared by the Federal Writers' Project of the Works Progress Administration between 1936 and 1941. Houghton Mifflin Company, Boston, and Oxford University Press, New York.

The White Pine Series of Architectural Monographs, Published by Russell F. Whitehead, Marchbanks Press, New York, 1918–1931 (out of print).

INDEX